THE ENDEARING ADVENTURE

BY

BLISS KNIGHT

TABLE OF CONTENTS

The Endearing Adventure 1

A Rosebud Sunrise 34

Alice 37

Sagittarius 38

Leader Emergence 39

Assessing the Interview 45

Leadership 50

Authority Without Wisdom 53

Herwig 58

Our Horses are our friends 60

Perpetrators 62

2009 64

Adventuring Spirit 65

Flying Air Tankers and the Robotic AI 69

Echoes of Life 72

DEDICATION

To those who have the courage to follow their dreams.

ACKNOWLEDGEMENTS

My history teacher at Yavapai College, Prescott, Arizona, who ensured I got historical events correct in their interpretation for the future.

ABOUT THE AUTHOR

1966 Associate of Arts, Foothill College, Los Altos Hills, CA., English classes, SF State University, classes in History at University of California, Berkeley; San Mateo College aviation academics, Alameda College A&P; Flight Safety International training Private through Airline Transport incl MEL and CFIs. 1964-1969.

Old Dominion University, Newport News, VA. Bachelor of Science in professional English and Meteorology, mostly online, in 2010. MBA from Western Governors University in 2014, gave the Commencement Speech on Value of Online Learning, available on YouTube.

1976 hired as line pilot by Western Airlines. Accomplished Turbine Flight Engineer Certificate.

1984 - 1994 FAA Designated Pilot Examiner: PVT-ATP, CFI ASMELI.

1985 checked out as FE on DC-10.

1987 Delta Air Lines bought Western Airlines, I checked out as second-in-command international on Lockheed 1011 Tri Star flying across the Pacific and Atlantic to European and Russian destinations. Boeing 737 Captain's rating.

Retired early from airline flying to sail Inland Passage SEA-JNU with my husband on his yachts for 12 years.

Accomplished USCG Inland and Offshore Masters License for 300,000 lbs ships.

I have no children and am now a widow living on my ranch in the shadow of the Sierras with my treasured animals.

THE ENDEARING ADVENTURE

When I am an old lady dressed in purple, reclining on my front porch swing, watching horses graze in their field of lavender grasses, I don't want to be wishing what I could have done with my life. Rather, I want to be reminiscing about the things I did do... my champagne-colored Irish Wolfhound, Odessa, reclines at my feet. She is lovely - has an inquisitive nature - and quietly walks by my knee, tail swaying with each step of her long body. If I should misstep when walking on uneven ground, she allows me to regain my balance by halting with my heavy hand on her back. She is one of many dogs I have had through the years, each one a willing partner: Great Danes, a Collie, Scotties, Newfoundlands, and now, an Anatolian Shepherd whom I call Leo.

Leo came from Genoa, Nevada, with the name of Lennon, given by his late, previous owner for the famous Beatles, whom he represented and promoted around the world, as well as other musicians like Fleetwood Mac and Kenny G. Leo is black, heavily though trim-coated, and weighs about 140 pounds. He arrived via friends who looked out for him – he needed a home. They thought we would be a happy pair, and we have been. He has a fierce bark, and ever since he arrived, my feral Persian Tomcat, Lou, has disappeared. I miss Lou, my partner.

My preference has always been large dogs, though once upon a time, I had a small Carin Terrier given to me by a friend whom the dog would not tolerate. Oatsy Muffin knew Friend was responsible for shooing her favorite Red away. Red, with his colorful mop and mustache tips sweeping inches past the perimeter of his cheeks, famous for his aerial exploits, had been her lover for a quarter. He and his family lived near anchorage, and Red kept airplanes in a hangar at Wien on the Water. Once, he rescued his pilot arrested for smuggling, plucking him from a Mexican prison yard by helicopter, though he neither told nor acknowledged the story was true. It was a story that just followed him around. That was in the glory days of Western Airlines, America's oldest airline, one that was brave enough to hire me, a woman, as a pilot.

Though I was surrounded by men in my career, I hadn't been in a relationship for years until I met my new husband. I dated a lot and eventually came around to thinking that there was something of value in having the correct relationship with a man: a future, perhaps children, and time spent compatibly. Ten years had elapsed since my last marriage. I hadn't met a man whom I wanted to marry. I preferred to adventure alone.

I needed to buy a home and get out of California, which had such high income taxes. The first year after probation with the airline, when my salary quadrupled, I had to borrow money to pay my California state income taxes. I gave my substantial down payment savings to my sister and her husband when he asked me to help pay for his medical school. I took serious note that he had single-handedly built and sold a lovely mountaintop home in Marin County with views of San Francisco, but the proceeds didn't quite cover his expenses. The 60 medical schools he applied to would not accept him because he was almost 30 years old, though he had graduated with honors from Stanford University with a Bachelor's Degree in Pre-Med. He eventually did become a doctor, graduating from the first outlaw medical school in the Caribbean situated on the volcanic island of Montserrat. Once in practice, he paid me back with a much-appreciated interest of 20 percent, though in trying to compliment my sister for them doing what I never expected - paying me back at all - she took exception to what she thought was an insinuation that they would not honor their word. This was not my intent - just to congratulate them on their diligence, and we did not part well.

So, having given away my down payment, I reluctantly entered a partnership with my parents after extensive negotiations. We bought a lovely home in Nevada just over the Sierras from Lake Tahoe in the beautiful Carson Valley. They would make the big down payment, and I would make the substantial monthly payments. This arrangement would benefit me at tax time, and for that, I was grateful.

Now, I would have someone to eat dinner with and talk to on my days off from flying for the airline, though I spent most of my time alone. I bought a nice horse for riding and a Great Dane for companionship and developed an association with a flight school at the Minden - Tahoe Airport – MEV. I took up gliding. Soaring the Sierra Wave was an action to look forward to...beautiful views of the mountains and Lake Tahoe, and someday, entering worldwide soaring competitions. This would give me a reason to travel, and I looked forward to the adventure.

In exchange for lessons in a glider, I towed glider pilots to areas of lift with a Piper Pawnee or the French Rally. I checked out in Evergreen's Lockheed P2V air tanker at MEV. Based on my experience dropping smoke jumpers for a parent company, Intermountain Aviation, out of Marana, Arizona, I was considered eligible and became the first woman to receive in 1981 an Initial Attack Rating on fires from the US Forest Service, a coveted laurel. Homeowners waved from their rooftops with garden hoses in their hands as we flew on by dropping fire retardant. Colored red and easily spotted by other attack planes, Fos-check and Fire Stall are taffy-like fertilizers that encourage new growth.

I was genuinely touched to be spending time with my aging parents. We traveled some and got to visit places in the world we always wanted to see using my airline passes. But after a year, we ran out of places, and when I arrived home from my airline trips, I was astonished to find that my mother was at a girlfriend's for the night. This left me alone with my dad...at first, I wasn't sure what to make of this situation. I felt awkward and at odds. When this repeatedly happened, I began to understand more than I really wanted to...then, my parents went to Yosemite for a weekend, staying at the Ahwahnee Hotel with friends. Shortly after they left, their lifelong friends knocked on my front door. They said they knew that my parents were in Yosemite and had driven up from Monterrey to speak with me.

I was quite taken that they would go to such effort on my behalf as it was some distance: I listened carefully to what they had to say. Mother told them she was hoping to reinforce my financial commitment to our partnership by leaving me alone with Dad... I had been wondering if there wasn't something more, if I wasn't missing something, and I acknowledged to this couple that spending all my time alone made me feel incomplete.

I began considering finding a male companion, a husband. Not that I needed someone to support me; I never considered myself a Chattel, but it would be nice to have a companion. Coupling was an acceptable way to spend time and be admitted to social circles. A single person, an attractive woman of eligible age, was a threat, and I was not invited to join. Hence, I spent most of my time alone. Alone at work at the airline, where male bonding – but not with me - occurred during flights and extended to layovers; alone on days off, at my shared home in Nevada, I spent most of my time riding my horse or flying, towing gliders, or flying them. My frame of mind began to change to the possibility of getting married again. Now, I just needed to find the right man, and that would be no easy task. I was coming up on forty, and it seemed that most of the good men were taken. Finding one that excited me, whom I could trust to hold up his end, whom I could fall in love with would be no easy task - a quest in itself. But ever the optimist, I was sure I could find the right one for me. There had been numerous contenders, but none I could go the distance with.

As my mother often spoke about the wealth and success of her father, Wallace Price, I was curious about my maternal roots and kept vigilant when information came my way. Perhaps because of her early circumstances, Pattie was given to making more of things than was there and was acutely aware of her place - or the lack of - in society. Her father started Hills Brothers Coffee. He was supposed to have opened trade with China by first importing tea and spices with his sailing ships in the 1880's. Among his possessions was Signal Hill, with its bounty of oil. He belonged to the Masons, and when his first wife died, he married my maternal grandmother, Helen Wood. She was a member of the feminine equivalent of the Masons, the Eastern Star, which was how they met. Helen graduated from the University of Washington when women rarely went to college but was financed by her prospecting father, who sent money home to his growing family living on a houseboat on Lake Washington. He prospected during the gold rush in Alaska.

Wallace Price was much older than Helen. In fact, she was younger than his youngest child. There were four children: a daughter, Ione, and three brothers, one of whom was Virgil Price. My mother, Pattie, was the only child born from that late union. Wallace bought his sons the racetrack when they showed up late for a car race – the only way for them to compete. When he died, he gave his sons everything. Helen was left with Pattie and a large house of 28 rooms in the Oakland hills near Piedmont. She had to open the house to boarders to make ends meet. Pattie and Helen took on cleaning and sewing. Among their boarders

4

was Helen's younger bachelor brother, Edmund, whom we called Empy. Uncle Empy was the Assessor for the City of Oakland and wrote long letters to us while on vacation, traveling around the world via freighters. He invested heavily in silver and left his substantial investments to my mother when he died. She used the money to our advantage by helping us into a more elegant home in Los Altos Hills near Stanford University and to start her EMF Company. Uncle Empy's stories about his travels enthralled me, and his letters about his adventures abroad may have been influential in developing my yearning to travel and see the world.

When my mother married Adellon Hanson, Dell, as he was called, she began a way of life dotted by moving and changes, all to her liking as she had an adventuring spirit and she liked being the Colonel's wife. He graduated from the University of California in Electrical Engineering partly on a football scholarship and mostly through hard work. "Moose" Hanson had to quit football in his junior year because school was so tough, and just before Cal went to the Rose Bowl!

He lumber jacked in Wisconsin in the summers and dug ditches – so his mother thought - for the Oakland Water Company in the winter. But the pay was better welding the Bay Bridge underwater as a hard hat diver. He said, "It's good to keep your pump man in your corner because he needs to keep turning that wheel!" When he graduated from CAL, the Second World War was just beginning, and he was commissioned as an officer in the Regular Army. There were three of these elite spots available. He got one of them by scoring highly on a competitive examination. The military recognized his potential and sent him to the University of Pennsylvania, Harvard, and MIT, where he completed his master's degree in EE and helped Werner Von Braun develop space technology; Dell's minor was Astronomy. He told me about a then-secret: Radar. Dad was a positive influence in my life, and as the oldest of his children, he took me hunting and fishing and taught me the way of the woods while he was stationed at the Army's Cold Weather Test Station in Big Delta, Alaska. When he wanted to learn to fly while he was Satellite Systems Test Director at Lockheed in Sunnyvale – soon to be Silicon Valley - I was tickled to be his instructor. I recalled that early on, when I related my instructor aspirations, he commented: "Flight instructor?! Who in the world would want to learn to fly from You!"

5

It was a memorable day for me when I soloed him. True to his nature, he then progressed to his Commercial Certificate, with Instrument and Multi-engine ratings, while developing and flying the first geosynchronous orbital satellite, Agena, for Lockheed Missiles and Space in Sunnyvale.

He and my mother founded EMF Company in Mountain View. Highly technical, EMF stood for Electromagnetic Filter, and they designed and constructed these electronics along with filter interference devices and shielded test enclosures. My younger brother, Greg, traveled the world setting up testing facilities and even got to meet Jimmy Doolittle on a moose hunting trip in Alaska. EMF was a place for my brothers and sister to work while growing up and attending school. As the oldest child, I was already flying professionally as an instructor and never became involved with EMF. My mother saw this choice as offensive as EMF was one of the premier companies in Silicon Valley and was later sold to Precision Instruments. Mom was the owner and office manager of EMF as well as president of several organizations, including Amelia Earhart's Zonta, an organization for professional women. Although she was, as my dad put it, "a natural born leader," an efficient manager who ran things well, it didn't matter what the organization was or did. She provided the framework and machinations to get it done.

Dad was innovation. When he successfully designed and flew the Agena satellite, Lockheed offered him a Vice Presidency in Houston. I well recall his proud announcement at the dinner table and the disarming, life-changing responses he received: "Do we have to move again?!" "We just got here!" The upshot of it was that we didn't move as we had so many times before, sometimes every nine months and that this signaled an end to my dad's career with Lockheed. Sure, they transferred him around from department to department as manager, but after launching the first synchronous orbital satellite – confirming that satellites could be used for communications, not just the gathering of information - and fulfillment of a lifelong dream of working to develop technology in space, he was done.

He tried other things, accounting and design for EMF - but that was mom's deal - and cattle ranching in the beautiful Spanish Peaks area of Colorado - where he had to learn to ride a horse, and developmental design for Virgil Price, my mother's half-brother's silicon gravel pit named Broad Hollow

Estates, adjacent to Idlewild Airport on Long Island. But for the most part, he was done working.

When I arrived home to be with family, my parents were glad to see me. I had accomplished not only a milestone by becoming one of the first four women to be hired as a pilot for a major scheduled airline, Western Airlines, America's first airline, but I was also single. Divorced from my first husband, who could not tolerate my success nor my being away overnight and flying in the company of men, I was the first person to be divorced in my immediate family. I was free of emotional encumbrances. I spent nearly all my time alone.

Making a considerable salary, I had to borrow to pay my California State Income Taxes when my income quadrupled the first year after successfully completing the probationary period. My father offered a solution: move to Nevada, where there were no state income taxes. He also offered a solution to my loneliness: a partnership with my parents in a lovely home. We found one in the Carson Valley in Nevada, just over the sierras from Lake Tahoe. I would have company on days off, and they would care for a dog. I chose Pie`dade`, a female black Great Dane puppy sold to me by Isabel Steiner Karkau. Pie`dade` was the sweetest canine companion and went everywhere with me, riding in the backseat of my Honda Accord. Isabel owned a Great Dane kennel in Los Gatos and, years before, became my friend and mentor. She was in the third class of women pilots at the WASP training facility in Sweetwater, Texas, during WWII and mostly ferried pursuit fighters to bases abroad for deployment in Europe. Having attended Stanford University, she was the first woman there to graduate with a Master's degree in Mechanical Engineering. She flew her pink Stinson Reliant to school and joined the flying club. Years later, she completed a second master's degree in genetics at Stanford. We spent time together, and she encouraged me in my ventures. I accompanied Isabel to Senator Barry Goldwater's award ceremony at the Antlers Hotel in Colorado Springs in 1977, where he retroactively gave national homage to and the overdue GI Bill of Rights benefits to those women who aided their country as Women Air Service Pilots during the Second World War.

My arrangement with my parents was okay for a while, but I grew restless for companionship my own age. One day, arriving from a scheduled rotation to New York, I hurried across the ramp dressed in airline uniform - before the days of airport security - to my commute flight home to Reno, parked at the departure gate. Ascending the ramp stairs, I entered the jetway and joined the back of a line waiting for access to the airplane cabin. Suddenly, there were big footsteps coming down the jetway hall, and I turned to see my next husband...

Juan Noche` as his friends called him, was a hunk. Well over six feet tall, dressed warmly in a brown suede jacket and cashmere sweater with chest hair protruding from the "V," he cut an imposing figure. When he directed a greeting of "Gooood Morning!" To me, in a booming voice, I decided he was worth a second look. We began by conversing about the airplane manual he held in his hand: the Cessna Conquest. I commented that I had flown its predecessor, the Turbo Star, at Scenic Airlines. I noted that after long days of flying recipes with the ensuing vibrative fatigue permeating my body, turbines were a smooth and welcome relief.

He agreed.

As we progressed in the line towards the door, I enjoyed his voice, impressively deep and full. He had naturally beautiful teeth and a broad smile. Our turn came to sit, and we went to our respective seats. I was in First Class, and he was in Coach on the aisle, just behind the bulkhead separating the two cabins. I waited until we were airborne to ask the Senior Flight Attendant: "May I invite a man I have just met to sit with me?" He responded: "That would be fine as there are few passengers in First Class." I stepped into the forward lavatory to change out of my uniform and into a seasonal orange silk blouse, took down and ran a comb through my long dark hair, then stepped back to ask Juan if he would like to sit with me.

I noticed his strong profile as we talked. I was really into noses, and he was a straight one. He had large, somewhat rough hands and big feet tucked into nice loafers. These physical attributes were noteworthy, but what was really impressive was his voice. It was full of confidence. Juan Noche` was a commanding package. He said he had been single for years.

He asked me to dinner at the Pink House in Genoa that evening. He was meeting the Nevada State Criminal Investigator and his wife for dinner... I explained that the Pink House was my hangout after gliding – one of the reasons I chose to live in this part of the world: to soar the Sierra Wave. The Pink House was originally a staging place for wagon trains traveling across the Sierras. Frequently headed by Kit Carson and Hank Monk, I was sure I could hear the rustle of horses in harnesses and wagons outside while we dined inside by the fireplace of that mansion in Nevada's oldest town. A year later, we had our wedding reception there.

I spent the summer in training on Western's new DC-10. The aircraft had a Flight Engineer, and my seniority allowed me to bid for and secure this position. Ground school classes were during weekdays with weekends off, and this weekend, I was going to Tucson to meet Juan. He was picking me up at the airport in his Aero Star, and we were flying onto Cabo San Lucas to meet his friend John Lyndon and go whale watching aboard his Don Juan. Just off the point of Cabo, Humpback Whales were breeching, tail-walking on the water, showing off for potential mates. In due course, one swam alongside the boat and, at somewhere around 40 feet, lay on its side looking up at us with its large round eye. Barnacles clung to its cheeks, and his color was dark, iridescent green. The thrill of petting this whale sent rapturous waves of discovery up and down my body.

When I arrived back in class on Monday, a fellow trainee remarked on my sun-kissed appearance: "Great! While we hung around the hotel studying all weekend, you were on a boat in Mexico working on your tan!"

I fell for Juan but was mystified by his midnight gasps for air, which caused him to sit erect in bed. He made a terrible racquet trying to catch his breath. Sometimes, this occurred during the day if he had eaten chocolate or enjoyed a martini. I was alarmed, but he brushed it off.

It was my Birthday the next day, December 3. We departed Gatwick, leaving the coast of England, climbing out over Brighton Beach, and headed for Cincinnati in the US. Passing Greenland about halfway across the North Atlantic with its shoreline of calving icebergs and mountainous blue snow, silently, I thanked the powers-that-be for the spectacular view from the flight deck of our elegant conveyance, Delta's Flagship, the Lockheed 1011-500, the airplane I now flew regularly somewhere in the world as second-in-command. My husband would be meeting us on arrival, and we were going to celebrate my birthday together. We planned to have a nice dinner at the top of a nearby hotel with a view of the city. Juan ate lamb and me, Veal Oscar, a medium-rare beef filet topped with lobster, asparagus, and hollandaise sauce.

I had a surprise for our day off together in Kentucky. As we gazed out across the city lights dappled by snowflakes, I related how, on board, I met a reporter for Horse and Hound. He was pleased to be flown by a female flight officer involved in horses and offered his visitor spot at the Shadwell Breeding Farm in Lexington, Kentucky, for my Birthday celebration, owned by Mohammed bin Rashid al Maktoum, a Sheik and Royal famous for his Thoroughbred racing horses, he was also Vice President and Prime Minister of the United Arab Emirates and Ruler of Dubai.

The next day, we rented a car and drove to Lexington. Arriving at the imposing gates of the farm, a dark but pleasant guard stepped forward to greet us. My contact had phoned ahead, and the farm manager was expecting us. We entered through reception, and the first thing to greet us was an enormous oil painting hanging over a crackling fireplace. It was of a large company of men mounted not on horses but on camels. I thought, how strange, this is a horse breeding farm, and these men are riding camels! They were all bearded and grinning, wearing turbans, clothed in white linen blouses and beige jodhpurs. "To my brother, Maktoum el Maktoum, from your brother, Maktoum el Maktoum," was inscribed at the bottom. He was the only man in the picture without a beard.

We toured the farm. Each barn was a round brick building surrounded by several acres of Kentucky bluegrass where mares and young foals grazed, the reason the Sheik chose Kentucky. An Overseer was elevated on a platform above the horses, a computer screen pointed at each stall. A weaned foal, usually bay in color, groomed and exercised, stood calmly, elegantly, in the center with ears perked as if this was his job.

When my husband commented on the quality of the leather halter given to each colt, the manager explained they had no budget. The Sheik flew his horses to races all over the world but usually to Europe - in one of his transports, a DC-8 or B747, and became famous for having paid the most -$7M – for a yearling colt. We enjoyed our tour and arrived home with new ideas but on a more moderate scale.

It was a memorable day when my new husband of two months divulged that he couldn't have any more children. Having a child was one of the reasons why I consented to marry again. This gave me pause as it was news to me that I would not have a child married to Juan Noche`. "Couldn't you have this reversed?" I asked in an encouraging voice, noting that many of the fellows I flew with had, resulting in children. He explained that he had had an early vasectomy, and it was irreversible.

This was a defining moment for me. For a time after this revelation, I considered getting pregnant by another man or calling this marriage off. Why would he not have discussed this with me earlier when we were an item? It made me think a whole lot less of him and was an epiphany for me in that it gave clarity to my feelings for him.

Withholding this information seemed unfair, just as asking me to sign a prenuptial agreement one week before our wedding ceremony. He caught me by surprise then, just as he did now. I was deeply disappointed in the man. From all appearances, this was not in his character, but I was finding out what was missing. He had no honor. This flaw made him less appealing and gave mount to my misgivings. I gave this much thought.

Though sorely disappointed, I took to breeding warm-blooded horses instead of having children. After all, how could I be leaving town with a sick or lonely child back at home? To have another person hear my child's first word or watch a first step was unfathomable! Oh well, I sighed. I probably didn't need the distraction of children while flying internationally for Delta, anyway.

11

We hadn't flown the Westwind for over a year - since we got our type ratings to fly the corporate jet - but today, my husband's adventuring spirit perceived we had a window of opportunity. We would fly it to Casper to his hunting ranch in the Medicine Bow Mountains of Wyoming. It was a preparatory outing to get ready for the elk hunt in the fall.

Over my protests, Juan put me in the left seat with the admonishment: "Well, you are the jet pilot..." True, I was flying the Lockheed 1011 Tri-Star internationally for Delta Air Lines - my normal job during the week, but the Westwind was a very different type of jet: a corporate version that did not even have reverse thrust of the engines for stopping. If the brakes were not enough, there was a deployable emergency parachute. Needless to say, I would be on high key during takeoff!

After a weather briefing, we filed an instrument clearance to be picked up en route as there was no clearance delivery on the ground - nor a tower - at the Provo Airport near my ranch in Spanish Spanish Fork. Departing the longest runway - Juan hadn't gotten the radios working yet, and he was all arms and elbows searching the cluttered overhead panel for the one last knob an arm's length above and behind him.

I climbed out steeply to maintain the mandatory 250 knots speed below 10,000 feet - a speed which allowed for the mix of traffic in congested areas and diminished bird strike damage, should it occur. Over the town of Springville, I had to level off at 17,500' before penetrating Positive Control Airspace above, as we didn't yet have our instrument clearance. Our requested cruising altitude was FL 270 – with the altimeter set at 29.92" mg - approximately 27,000 feet. Momentarily, Juan got our radios working, copied our instrument clearance, and I resumed our climb. Leveling off a couple of minutes later, I took a deep breath, looked around at the magnificent Uinta Mountains below, and relaxed until TOD - top-of-descent. Then Juan took the wheel...

He departed our cruising flight level with a high rate of descent and airspeed within 10 knots of the red line. As we passed 17,500' on the way down, Juan slowed to 250 knots and said: "Let's say hello to our ranching friends!"

He canceled our instrument clearance and proceeded visually: eyeballs to

Casper. Inbound, he mostly flew at less than 100 feet AGL – above ground level – around hills, down little valleys, and over several different ranch houses. We didn't have a chance to see if anyone stepped outside as we were closing in on the Casper Airport. Juan gave over control to me as it was to be my landing. I managed a smooth touchdown and we taxied to the terminal.

The engines were shutting down, depressurizing the cabin, then the cockpit secured. The ground attendant was given a thumbs-up - my all-clear signal that we were depressurized, and he was free to open our passenger door. The only passenger, our black Newfoundland dog, Green Meadow Bear, sat elegantly in the center of the curved leather aquamarine-colored divan at the rear, balancing with his front feet on the floor. He was a big, good dog and went anywhere I went if allowed. As the door opened, he leaped out over the astonished attendant's head onto the red carpet leading to the front door of the terminal and trotted over to a rosebush heavy with yellow blooms...

One of the things Juan confided to me on this trip while we played Chess was his wish to drive a four-in-hand. I thought I could help set things in motion by giving him a black Percheron driving horse named "Bud" for his 60th birthday. With Bud came his trainer, Chief Jim Wilson. He became our driving - and my riding instructor. Chief was a retired Chief Warrant Officer in the U.S. Army and a great-grandson of Chief Crazy Horse of the Lakota Nation - commonly called by white folk - the Sioux.

The stories Chief told in mornings over coffee while we waited - for the horses to finish eating and low clouds to clear - were fascinating. As a young man of fifteen, living with his parents on their ranch outside the Lakota reservation at Rosebud, South Dakota, he drove a team of four to six Percherons every early winter morning to feed the cattle while his father drove a team of Clydesdales - in the opposite direction. In summer, the cattle ate grass. When young Jim joined the US Army Cavalry at the end of WWI, he rode horses and drove draft horse teams to position artillery pieces on the battlefield. When the Second World War broke out, the cavalry was absorbed into the artillery, and the horses retired.

When Hitler captured the Spanish Riding School as a prize and made off with 100 Lipizzaner stallions to Yugoslavia with the Russians closing in, General Patton ordered that the Academy horses should be rescued before the Russians could take control. Chief was chosen by General Patton as one of five past reputable cavalry riders to parachute silently from a transport glider on a moonlit night. Their mission was to capture and ride the Lipizzaner Stallions back into the Austrian Hills. Each man carried a bridle and a sack of oats in his backpack. When the mission was successfully completed, and the destructive war was over, the Spanish Riding School invited Chief to attend. He refined his riding technique over the next two years from the instruction given him there by Masters in Dressage. I was fortunate to meet Chief and have him as my Driving Instructor and Dressage trainer.

For years, we broke my young warm-blood horses and taught the evenhanded ones to drive. When Chief sadly died in his mid-eighties, Juan found an Amish boy who could both train and drive horses as he did on his father's farm. We collected 10 hitch-type horses, which differed from the farm type in that their front leg action began at the shoulder rather than at the ankle. Together, this gave them a harmonious, fancy, energetic appearance. We outfitted them with patent-leather dress harnesses and transported them around the country to competitions in the custom Exiss horse trailer Juan had built. He pulled them with a new Freightliner truck, and I drove the 42-foot Monaco Camelot Motorhome, pulling the 38-foot cargo trailer containing two carriages and the triangular, wheeled structure of hanging harnesses. One carriage was a fancy, high-wheeled red and black sulky - driven by a single person - designed to show a single horse. The other was a handmade wagon of maple with six horse hitches carved on the front, back and sides. I was very proud of the quality of our wagon as it was indeed a work of art and the finest I had ever seen. Pictures of them now line my halls.

At 20, young Rudy wasn't old enough to be insured to drive either of the rigs, so the driving fell to Juan and me. Our Percheron Hitch did well at shows. Rudy, Juan, and I drove the multiples, and I drove my Woody in the ladies' classes around the country, most notably winning the Ladies Hitch Championship in a field of 17 in Auburn, California, in 2009 - my very first show driving Percherons!

14

It is the summer of 2009, and my husband and I are aboard our boat, the 48-foot Eclipse sport fishing boat "Flyer," so named because it is fast. At 25 knots, we are exploring a remote Tlingit Reservation backwater in southeast Alaska. It has taken a couple of hours to get to this area from our accommodation in Hoonah. For what reason we have come, he has not let me know, except that now he is circling a 20 x 20' isle, insisting that he wants to take a picture of me by the totem pole projecting from the center. The tide is out, and the totem is tall with its red and black carved figures, but when the tide is in, the carved pole protrudes from the water by only a few feet.

Surely, he must know that I am aware of the tides, being that we finished our US Coast Guard Masters Licenses together. There would not be anywhere to stand without getting wet. And the water is cold, very cold. My inner sense of warning tells me not to exit the boat. Something is going on with him, and it is puzzling... this feeling forwards a warning to believe that my husband of 24 years would not allow me back aboard the boat but would leave me there... to be inundated by the rising tide. Trust is no longer something I can count on him for...But why? I do not get off the boat, though he is insistent that I do so for a picture...

I recognize an ardent persuasion in him that has not surfaced before. He is getting angry as I refuse over and over. Finally, he turns from the continuous circling of the isle and heads away from this lonely spot in the backwater of the reservation where a call for help would go unheard. For a moment, but only a moment, I breathe a sigh of relief. I am stunned and wonder why this mean action has taken place. Previous to this excursion, he spent several weeks with his son. It would be easy to explain that I got off the boat for a picture and disappeared in the rising water. There was nothing he could do... I am stunned and speechless as we speed back to Hoonah. Juan doesn't say a word. Suddenly, I knew that my husband was a dangerous man and that he could no longer be trusted.

Just off the point of land leading to the port, Humpback whales circle, blow bubbles, and drive a ball of fish to the surface. With huge mouths open to swallow, it is as if they are grinning and jubilant while I am so discouraged and on high alert!

15

With boats, we are in transition, as Flyer is to replace the larger Morning Mist due for an overhaul of its locomotive-size engines. It is very slow at 8 knots. Juan surprises me by remodeling the MM interior green and purple soft velour appurtenances with slick brown leather. This event alarms me as he has not included me in the decision, and the Morning Mist is supposed to be mine: he bought it for me some years ago and now has not consulted me about the remodel or sale!

We are in the process of building one home from two in Pelican - I have purchased many Alaskan furnishings for it. Pelican is a town with lovely cross-strait views of waterfalls cascading down the mountains. Pelican is a fishing village situated on a "bite" 100 miles in on the Lisianski Strait, southeast of the Icy Straits, where at the end of a day exploring, we could speed back to have overnight accommodation ashore instead of aboard. Relieved that at night, finally, I would not have to secure every aperture from bears who might swim out and climb on looking for food, I look forward to the change.

Pelican is easy to get to after a day on the route from our ranch in Arizona. Flying into Juneau in our Westwind or Solitaire, then boarding Wings, a seaplane taxi service out of Juneau that operates de Haviland Twin Otters on floats into and out of the Pelican Harbor, it is much faster than boating the 125 miles, especially after a long day flying from Arizona.

This is the tenth year we have been departing the ranch in early May and flying to Juneau until the end of September, when it starts to get cold. Our animals are cared for by Tito, Hector Gonzalez, our ranch foreman - who trained and rode for Bob Baffert, winner of many triple crowns, and Tito's crew, though I miss all of them.

I ponder this unusual behavior in my husband, which has been prevalent and growing ever since his genetic cancer was confirmed in 2005. He has been keeping company more and more with the oldest son from his first marriage - mine was his third marriage - a son I taught to fly with our ranch Cessna 206 Skywagon - and whom I thought was good enough to solo from the ranch strip.

At 4,750 feet in elevation and surrounded by low hills, a 2000' x 20-foot strip can be a tight and exacting operation, even if it is paved. Tre was a good flight student, and I was a confident instructor, confident that he would rise to this challenge.

Tre's was a smaller version of his dad. At 6'2", with very blond hair and blue eyes, he is a reflection of his Teutonic and Catalonian ancestry. He dazzled me with his quick interpretation and solution to the Rubik's Cube, taking only about 10 seconds to configure the cube properly. He encouraged his father's attention over all his other children. I wondered if this affinity had something to do with the fact that Juan's father left Juan's mother when he was only three... Juan favored this son over all of his other children because he was a son, because of his nature, his aptitudes, and intelligence.

That Tre's had never really worked may have been the reason he pursued his wealthy father's attention. Inheritance is one way to acquire wealth without having to work. Once, Tre's worked for a winter on an exchange program for Siemens in Germany. When I asked him about this choice as I had read a treatise on how Siemens had initially prospered building Hitler's abattoirs - Tre's felt the company would be a good fit. I began to recognize Tre's for what he was: a predator. This was one explanation for a fellow who kept a 3-foot pet crocodile in his college bathtub while other students kept pets it would eat.

On summer break from school, Tre's paternal grandfather sponsored the aggressive Tre's in boxing with professional Las Vegas trainers. Tre's like going to the Fight Club whenever. It gave him a sense of belonging, something he apparently didn't feel... Grandfather felt that boxing was one way to make seed money. Ultimately, Tre's won the National Golden Gloves Middle Heavyweight Championship. He badly broke his opponent's jaw and, with a jab to the head, delivered a concussion. Visiting his opponent in the hospital seemed out-of-character for the champion, but Tre's gave the appearance of being touched by the havoc he had wrought; it gave him pause... there was a twist here: it was a way to give up boxing – Tre's didn't like being hit, so there must be an easier way - and for a reason his ardent grandfather could understand: compassion, a quality his grandfather had and often exhibited that Tre's distorted the facts of this event would become a hallmark of his disposition.

Tre's quit Siemens to go with a traveling circus as an assembler and a featured Slight-of-Hand. His Rubik's Cube alacrity translated to cards and other tricks. He traveled around Europe before Juan bought him a return ticket home to the United States. In return, Tre's was there to help and learn his father's business.

They kept each other's company, often for months at a time. At one point, Juan moved to West SW Phoenix and roomed with his son Tre's and his friend, a fighter pilot out of Luke AFB on F-16s. For six months, I didn't see much of my husband – he declined to help with our Three Day Sanctioned Zephyr Ranch Combined Training Event that we had held at our Utah ranch for years. It was the only Intermediate-level competition between the coasts, and the jump height was only a few inches shy of that of advanced courses.

I spent time in Europe studying the Royals' courses and arrived home with their course designer. It turned out to be a $70,000 investment, and notables like Olympian champions David and Karen O'Connor and New Zealand's Blythe Tait held clinics for competitors after my competitions.

Juan came home every few months: this time to buy equipment from the Army Depot at Tooele, located southwest of Salt Lake City near the Bonneville Salt Flats, where he previously partnered with Orlen Black and won the still-standing land-speed record with their rail. It had Nitrous Oxide Fuel Injection, which made it go faster and which race officials evidently didn't understand and so did not know or care about. I believe Juan got the idea from our round-the-world diving trips, where we used nitrous oxide in our oxygen tanks to improve our diving performance.

The equipment Juan bid on at the Army Depot was to construct a Separation Plant – a Refinery. Both diesel and gasoline fuels were transported on the Williams pipeline, which passed through Parker, Arizona, on its way east. It was sold cheaply at the rack as trans-mix, a pipeline interface - a combination of diesel and gasoline - which overlapped on the route because there were no separation pigs between the two products. One product drove the next and was a necessary means for transporting products on the pipeline.

This mixing presented a problem. The trans-mix was sold at the rack rather inexpensively – the major oil companies didn't want to deal with it - but if refined back to the individual products and sold, Juan recognized this could be a real bounty. Never mind that the trans-mix had high sulfur content, which would be illegal after regulations for over-the-road fuels changed to low sulfur only in Arizona in 2012. It was 1992, and that limitation was years away. His intent was to build a refinery that would process the trans-mix back into two products, gasoline, and diesel, and sold individually.

Juan, with me in trial, showed up at the Tooele Army Depot in 1990 without sufficient means to acquire the necessary equipment - he hadn't thought all the needed equipment would be there, but it was, and there were but a few of each. So, he was compelled by expediency to buy the needed equipment and not wait. We had not been to the area of Bonneville Salt Flats since his rail broke the World Land speed record with Orlen Black driving. At 6'4", Juan was too tall to fit in the cockpit. Just as he took the world championship uphill record in Jackson Hole with Donnie Brusco driving Juan's snowmobile, both vehicles used nitrous oxide injection for unbelievable speeds and power.

Now, looking at equipment to build his separation plant, Juan, embarrassed, shuffled his feet and harrumphed as he was financially unprepared. To complete his purchase of the 1950s equipment, he needed my help. I offered to let him use several of my airline credit cards with unlimited credit, and the transactions were complete. His financial squaring with me was something I assumed my husband would do but never did. He made occasional payments but was never consistent, so it took me twenty-two years to pay the balances. That I would benefit from the proposed structure by being his wife was given. The experiences were memorable; the proceeds accorded me a most lavish and adventuresome lifestyle, but it would have been better for me in the future if this transaction had been documented, as I have never been repaid.

After the purchases were complete, and as a thank you for helping to acquire the equipment immediately, Juan took me to a dive site on the Bonneville Salt Flats to check out in a Dry Suit. We were going to be diving in Alaska's cold water. Experienced Nitrous Oxide Divers, we dove around the world, meeting friends who also had the time and means.

Neptune Divers of Tooele employed the use of deep volcanic tubes and caverns filled with warm volcanic water where the staff planted tropical fish. Invited by friends John and Gloria Buchan - home developers from Seattle - aboard their boat to have the new experience of dry suit diving, we motored with them to a picturesque spot off the coast of British Columbia called the Aquarium.

At first, I had a difficult time getting down below the surface until Juan descended and came back up with several fist-sized rocks he put in my pockets. The underwater scenery was enchanting - so many colorful lichens, coral, and small fish. I looked around: there was a huge Halibut - the size of a barn door - resting on a ledge above a precipice, waiting for a good fish to swim by. Suddenly, the many fish scattered as if afraid. Later, on board, I believe I hooked into that large Halibut. Trying to boat the colossus proved too much for the equipment - a twenty-pound test line - and I had to let him go...then I noticed a large pod of Orcas cruising along the coast in an inverted "V" formation. Their dorsal fins were up vertically because they were free, and the lead was much higher than the others. They scared everything in their path. There would be no fishing tonight...

The plant was built to Juan's specifications and became operational in six months with the 1950s technology – high sulfur fuel products would be produced and still could be sold in Arizona and used for over-the-road travel, at least until not allowed after January of 2012. Like one of my brothers, Doug, and his son, Jeff, who initially ran the place, mechanics would have to bend wrenches and take an active part in making the plant operate by physically opening and closing transfer valves.

It took nearly a year of constant work to get the refinery up and running with crews Juan flew in each Sunday evening from Utah in his Mitsubishi Solitaire. With a quick stop in Flagstaff to load/unload workers, I worried about the winter weather in Flagstaff as the airport is over 7,000 feet in elevation and had a non-precision approach with a circle-to-land procedure. And snow – so much snow – had to be cleared from the runway to allow flight operations.

These things proved to be no problem for Juan, who was really good at flying basics as well as instrument flying. He was a general aviation pilot with many thousands of hours. Having begun flying a Piper Cub at seventeen, he developed a feel for flying and had what pilot friends called "good hands," an ability to maneuver smoothly but with knowledge and coordination.

When we met, one of our first serious dates was to visit his truck stop in Kingman. He explained that he was always working. He picked me up after my airline rotation at the Salt Lake International Airport in his Super Star, a highly modified version of Ted Smith's Aero Star. It was early spring, and on this day, there was inclement weather: snow in SLC and blowing in Kingman. This was to be the first of our many flights over the years.

I was impressed when he picked up his instrument clearance - from air traffic control, read it back, and executed the flight perfectly. We proceeded to take off from SLC in snowy conditions and climb in the clouds to our assigned cruising altitude - this was something it took a flight crew to accomplish at the airline. We were on top of the overcast at 22,000 feet. He secured the de-icing equipment, which was not needed above the clouds in visual flight conditions. Then he put his arm around me and began one of his endearing conversations...

I asked what FAA Certificates he held while looking intently into his sky-blue eyes. He answered that he had a Private Pilot's license with Instrument and Multi-engine ratings. I took the opportunity to suggest that with the sophistication of this airplane, he should consider upgrading to the next logical flight certificate to help with his insurance rates: first, a Commercial single engine, and then an Airline Transport multi-engine because the ATP had to be preceded with a Commercial License. These were things that I could do for Juan Noche, a man I was becoming interested in, as an instructor and, ultimately, as an FAA Designated Pilot Examiner. I was not easily impressed. I was also a pilot, and at present, working as a pilot for Western Airlines.

At more than six feet tall, Juan was ruggedly handsome, well-spoken, and charming in a nice way - a commanding package. I was accustomed to commanding men – I was, after all, the Colonel's daughter, and I flew with commanding men, but here was one in the world of business, something I knew very little about until completing a Master's Degree in Business from Western Governors University in 2013, where I gave a commencement speech on the Value of Online Education. I am giving the speech in a YouTube presentation.

He told me how he bid for and got the fuel concession in Newport Harbor in the early sixties. He was in the oil business then, with tanker trucks he drove and a yard to keep them in. As a sideline, he cleaned barnacles and crustaceans off by using diving gear to scrape the bottoms of customers' boats. It was faster to use underwater breathing apparatus than hauling the boat out of the water. It took several tanks to complete the job. His father had bought tanks from Jacques Cousteau, a Frenchman who regularly came to Southern California to promote his innovative Aqua Lung.

Juan's fuel concession was an enormous success, aided in part by the Hollywood handsome, very tall, blond fellow in swim gear, who regularly dove in the harbor with an Aqua Lung on his back to clean the bottoms of boats. There were many onlookers. The fact was, Juan was the main attraction but didn't let it go to his head as he was making "seed" money for his next venture.

Juan's first wife left him and returned to her sisters. He loved his children and took legal steps to get custody of them. His new wife had two boys, and Juan would then have six children. The first wife implored Juan's father to help her keep her children. The custody battle spanned months in court. Juan was a loving father who wanted his children with him. The first wife was successful in her court bid for custody. Juan viewed his father's actions as a transgression – against his code of conduct - and did not have any contact with his dad for years. Dad had been a State Senator in California; in summers, he arranged for Juan to be a Page in the capital. This experience imparted confidence and sophistication in the young man.

Around the same time, a friend in the oil business who kept his yacht in Newport Harbor told Juan about Howard Morph, an investor who owned numerous old gas stations around Idaho. Juan flew to see Howard in Montecito, near Santa Barbara. Howard must have been impressed by Juan as the outcome of their meeting was that they formed a silent partnership: Howard would retain ownership of the properties and would finance Juan's updating of the gas stations by also creating convenience stores. The gas stations would be a better investment if modernized or heavily insured for loss. The ones that were not renovated somehow, in some way, became a loss.

22

With his second wife and her two sons, Juan moved from Kingman to Boise. We mutually agreed that the sign at the entrance to Kingman, which said, "Nigger don't let the sun set on you," was reason enough to leave. Juan spent holidays and vacations with his six children, usually in some activity involving water at Lake Powell or snow skiing in Aspen or Park City. The children flew with him to destinations where they could have fun and be together. They comprised Juan's social life.

When Juan sold the 28 True Value gas stations around Idaho, he also became the largest milk distributor in the state. So many times, customers asked for milk that he began selling it out of refrigerated glass cases in the convenience stores that now accompanied his gas stations.

He also spent a lot of time in court: True Value Hardware Stores objected to his use of their chosen name. Juan was able to keep the True Value name as he prevailed in court because his gas stations and convenience stores were not hardware stores. When Juan sold the gas stations, he and Howard got paid handsomely. Proceeds became seed money for Juan's next venture.

This was all accomplished during his second marriage, which lasted eight years. It meant time away from home, and his attractive wife took up with one of his managers in his absence... I kept vigilant but never badgered him as I took note that the second wife had. He said that she constantly woke him up during the night with questions about her portion of his money.

Finally, he left her at a distant motel when she became too insistent that he produce paperwork assigning her marital share of his holdings earned during their marriage. She had apparently divorced her first husband, the boy's father, to marry the attractive and ambitious Juan. Though he maintained her well during their marriage, he was apparently not given to ascribing marital paperwork, division of property, or payments for life insurance. These payments might limit his options and wealth, and having to be concerned about these accounts took up valuable time.

Early in our marriage, I received a letter from the chief pilot in Salt Lake City, who handed it to me. It was from this abandoned wife and detailed Juan's transgressions and contraventions. I thought it strange that she would resort to such tactics when I did not know her at all, but in retrospect, I knew it was to be regarded as a cautionary tale of what to look out for and what to expect. I read the typed, single-spaced, page letter standing by my locker with the Chief Pilot in my presence. That he should be concerned enough to deliver the letter in person was significant. He was notable in the Mormon Enclave and had once given me a ride to Juan's house near his own town. I looked into his eyes and saw genuine concern there; maybe he was familiar with Juan's reputation in the LDS church. At one time, Juan was up for president as he was so active. I later learned that he was excommunicated from the church, but I now suspect that he was threatened, then dismissed, because he would not give his wife her marital due.

I thanked the Chief Pilot, turned, and went on my way. I kept the warning in mind throughout the years of our marriage, and it served to modify my behavior and actions. When, for example, John Buchan communicated to me his concerns for my wife's welfare and financial future because Juan had indicated to him that he would not uphold the terms of our marital contract. I was somewhat taken aback, quite surprised, and speechless at this disclosure. Buchan was not really my friend or confidant. We were only just new acquaintances. I filed this away for future reference and, true to my nature, carried on as if nothing untoward had been revealed. Buchan then offered me rides in his airplane or boats to wherever he was going, and this gave me a sense of confidence and composure, but I had been alerted. Was this plan of my husband's obvious to all but me?

Always on the lookout for investments and in a business that he knew, Juan invested with two partners in an oil well drilling operation offered by JP Morgan in eastern Utah near Dinosaur National Monument. I read about this venture in the Salt Lake Tribune in 1984, shortly before I met Juan. Eventually, we visited the monument during a rafting trip on the Green River, and I was surprised by the extent and size of the excavations.

The sharp bend in the river served as an accumulative cache over a millennium. Several large dune-like extrusions were encapsulated by a rough roof-like structure protecting the archeologists' work. Excavations were noted by informative signage along the aisles as to the classification era of the discovery. In my experience, anywhere there were dinosaur remains and associated tar pits, there seemed to be oil, as in the La Brea Tar Pits in Santa Monica, California, so I anticipated that this drilling site selection was a good one, being that it

24

was in near proximity to this monument. I wondered about the ability of the investment house to secure such a drilling site. One weekend, Juan flew his two partners to the drilling site to see how the operation was progressing...to their surprise, when they arrived at the site, there was no activity. An old drilling rig lay, huge and idle, rusting on the ground.

It didn't take long to get a lawsuit filed with Attorneys Snow, Christensen, and Martineau of Salt Lake City against the popular investment house, as the take had been $2M each. Following the story in the Salt Lake Tribune, Juan Noche`, Verle Kruk, and D/arryl Prince reaped the benefit of winning back the money they invested as well as $15M split three ways. How to spend the money? They formed a partnership and built the largest chain of truck stops in the country during the 1970s using the innovative concept of networking, which assured support. The truck stops numbered between 48 and 52 and were built at intervals. Rounding a turn, thinking about fuel and food, and Bingo! There was a truck stop. Maintaining them became a drudgery as they always needed attention. Juan's partners were not given to venturing out by air away from their families as he was, and they were using up the ample returns to maintain their lifestyles. The time had come to collect the fruits of Juan's efforts: sell the truck stops and move on...

I was flying with Juan when he began selling the truck stops. We visited each of them by flying the potential buyers, individually, around the countryside in the Aero Star. The group east of the Mississippi sold to Sohio, west of the Mississippi in the Pacific Northwest to Burns Brothers out of Portland, and those in the southwest to Beacon Oil, a division of Ultramar out of London.

I would fly while Juan sold. In the end, sales negotiations chaired by attractive, independent businesswomen went well into the night and beyond to the wee small hours of the morning. They were fraught with calculations and verbal exchanges. There was a central meeting room and individual meeting rooms for the several entities. To be in on such goings-on was a new experience for me. Juan held my hand beneath the table throughout in anticipation of the outcome.

When the deal to sell the Bingo Truck Stops was concluded and the partners got paid, having so much money gave us pause. Juan began to consider the options. I found a full-page ad in the Wall Street Journal selling a million-acre cattle ranch in the northwest territory of Australia. With more than one hundred miles of oceanfront shoreline, six airplanes, lines of working cattle horses, crews of wranglers, houses, and boats, the operation had appeal for two adventurers such as we - it seemed an engaging operation, one that would be all-consuming. However, this venture would be life-changing. We would leave our home country and move to Australia. I would quit my coveted airline job...

When it came down to actually traveling there to see the operation, this gave us pause. In our hearts, we knew we would love the challenge and would probably be hooked. We decided that our lives were exciting enough, that we would miss our friends and families too much, and never went to see the ranch. Recently, I had the occasion to watch a program about the Northwest Territory of Australia on Nat Geo Wild. The area covered was the very area we had considered. The rancher was losing an alarming amount of cattle to "Salty," the saltwater crocodile that inhabits and has proliferated in the area for eons. Wranglers were contracted to helicopter-in enclosures baited with Ferrell pigs to catch and remove these large denizens to zoos. Hunting the Salties had been prohibited since 1971.

As part of the payment for the truck stop sales, Juan got the various operations on the Navajo Reservation and proceeded to build grocery and convenience stores, gas stations, a truck stop, a medical arts building, and later, a shopping center. He chose a Native American Chief, Wendell Mortenson, as his partner because business on the reservation required that one of the partners be First Nation, a Native American.

I couldn't understand how, when things took so long with what seemed endless negotiations and meetings, Juan could bear up, but he did and hung on well beyond my patience. What I realized later was that he had ulterior motives in mind that were beyond the arm of United States laws, which didn't exist on the reservation. I wondered when this change had occurred in him or if it had always been deeply hidden and, in my naiveté, I had not recognized the allusions. That he conceived a business so intricate and advantageous as designing and building a refinery by taking advantage of an available niche was a reflection of his complex personality. Wealth preservation and enhancement were his ends; exploration and adventure were his means.

I recognized a killer instinct in Juan's nature. I knew that he would use it if challenged. But Juan was disinclined to hurt anyone. Not that he wouldn't, but penalties for harming human beings were high, and incarceration could mean time away from the action, a roadblock to wealth accumulation. And so he contrived to use insurance companies.

He was insured and overinsured for losses on the reservation: buildings, warehouses, gas stations, grocery and convenience stores, medical arts buildings, and shopping centers. Each has a different insurance company and is insured to the max. Then, when the structure was destroyed or rendered unusable through some disaster or malfeasance, he would collect, put the money in his pocket, and not rebuild. Currently, this was how he made his seed money. In the case of the refinery, it would be rebuilt to state-of-the-art operations with collected insurance money from the buildings and structures destroyed. On the reservation, it was safer, as the arm of United States law was not present. It was a clever plan which took guts and skillful planning to implement.

I asked myself how and why a man with his talent and handsome looks, certainly a man among men, would resort to such deception when he could be good and play nicely. Never did he use the word *honor*, nor did he acknowledge the concept of being *honorable*. This gave me pause. It led to the ultimate realization that the man I was so in love with and married to did not consider *honor* as important... I wondered if ambitious, successful, wealthy men were saddled with the same shortfall.

In the rare instances of being with Juan's attractive, successful, and charismatic father, I found that he left Juan's mother because "she was a most vicious creature, and I found her presence intolerable!" That he abandoned his little family for an heiress left an indelible imprint on Juan's persona. When his father's heiress died many years later, he replaced her with Mary, whose father was Frank Noonan, the engineer on the first flyable airplane of the Wright Brothers' fame. Mary was Director of Welfare beginning when Hawaii became the fiftieth state on August 21, 1959, after Alaska, the 49th, on January 3 of the same year. She served in that capacity under three subsequent governors. John and Mary met at a social function in Honolulu, a favored location for the water-loving politician who swam or sailed each day along Waikiki Beach.

Like his father, Juan would not be like other people. For example, when I asked Juan why he did not go to college, he said he knew how to read, write, and calculate and didn't want to spend the time...college was for the working man... and Juan would never be in that harness.

He conceived a plan to design and build a refinery to separate pipeline petroleum interface – transmix – out of the shipped product. This mixing was a problem for the big oil companies as they used products to drive products through the pipeline. Juan planned to separate the transmix back to the original gasoline and diesel products.

He would buy transmix reasonably priced at the rack, refine it back into the two products, and sell it through his gas stations, truck stops, and future travel centers. By doing so, it had the potential of becoming a highly profitable vocation - a niche business. Transmix was a result of the two fuels, gasoline and diesel, overlapping, one driving the other through the pipeline. Without separation pigs between the products, this overlapping amounted to a problem for the large oil companies that transported fuels coast to coast on the Williams pipeline because, environmentally, the interface could no longer be dumped into bays, buried in the ground, or burned off into the air. And so this anomaly, transmix, was sold reasonably at the rack. Juan took this transmix, this pipeline interface, this problem, and refined it back to gasoline or diesel fuels at the refinery he built outside of Parker, Arizona, in less than six months with 1950s technology. The fuels had high sulfur content.

Juan wanted to upgrade the plant to 1990s technology by employing computers to open and close transfer valves instead of having to use mechanics bending wrenches. He contrived a plan to blow up the existing plant, which he had insured heavily with Lloyds of London, and make the modifications. Using stray gasses along the ground from a heater, part of the combustion event, his president, on duty that night, lit the heater, and boom! Blew up the plant.

Juan received the call in the wee small hours of the morning, and we hurried to the hospital to find his president severely injured, barely alive. His extended family was present, and from their interactions and treatment of us, I suspected that he had enlightened them as to the plan. What I couldn't understand was how someone, the president, who had knowledge of refineries, could light a heater when he knew there would be lingering gas fumes along the ground on a windless night. Damaged, he would reap millions and never have to work again.

The insurance company went for it, and the plant was rebuilt with state-of-the-art computers and technology controlling everything. There were years of litigation ahead, even extending to the federal level. Juan's attorney, Leo Beus, in an ensuing conversation with my lawyers and me in a conference call on a related matter, divulged that Juan had been awarded the highest amount paid to an individual by the federal government. By building this refinery, he had violated the Clean Air Act by potentially infusing high-sulfur products into the air. I was only aware of a $7M award, and at the time, I didn't think this was enough as the refinery had been shut down by the government; it had been the focus of our endeavors for so long.

The new refinery went on to make somewhere around $25M in four years leading up to the cessation of over-the-road high sulfur fuel usage in Arizona in 2012. Only ships at sea and trains could use high sulfur fuels, which I couldn't understand, as exhausted into the atmosphere - and when the air moves - is distributed over farmers' fields and enclaves of people, and was thought to be the genesis of disease such as cancers. And so the gas stations, truck stops, and travel centers were sold. The refinery was sold in 2012 without the low sulfur conversion for pennies on the dollar: the advantage vaporized just as the $25M+ made over the last four years had.

This money disappeared at the hands of Tre's and the operations manager, Verle Kruk. Though I employed a private investigating company to find out where offshore the money had gone, all they could find was that my husband had died of natural causes – heart failure. This was not believable as Juan had always had a healthy heart. It was an area of his body that was dependable. That he was cared for in a hospice where there was no coroner's report, only a death certificate, was a mystery as our divorce decree was forthcoming in only a few days, and the forensic report divulged several things...

I shared this information with a friend who was a registered nurse for the past 34 years. She boarded her horse with me and used the lights of my 175 x 225' indoor arena to ride dressage in the evenings after working all day. After her ride, she came in to warm by the fire, keep me company, and have a nightcap. She explained to me that insulin, given over several days intravenously, could bring on death and would be undetectable in an autopsy. It would be easy to administer as the equipment was already in place and medicines were being administered. She also verified that people who were in hospice did not necessarily have a coroner's attendance to verify how they had died.

I took serious note of this disclosure. She commented that Juan's death was coincidental with a forthcoming divorce decree as he died on a Friday, and the Forensic Investigation was to begin the following Tuesday. I was numb to the insinuation.

The Forensic Investigation did go through and took quite some time. The upshot of it was, and the document was more than 30 pages, that $25M was earned at the plant over the last four years before the plant was redefined. That bounty was most probably moved abroad and tax-free. Tre's was noted over and over in the document. He apparently dropped a single letter in his first name and changed a single number of his social security number, an action which remains unchallenged.

The same forensic investigation did not say where the money had gone, and a private investigation that lasted for months and months did not reveal the destination, either. I thought about all the free travel he had had through the years for only taxes, which were paid by me because of my airline association... it looked like I was not going to be repaid. Juan's promise to reimburse the professorial salary I was making as an Aviation Academics Instructor at Embry Riddle Aeronautical University in Prescott when he asked me to quit and go boating with him for ten years on the inland passage of Alaska was not going to happen, either. Nor would I be repaid for advancing my credit cards to buy the initial equipment for building the plant, which had taken me twenty-two years to pay off at $7000 per month.

The many residences which I furnished with my own money were a loss to me. I had assigned half of my ranch to Juan to ensure his cooperation in these money matters. In the process of our divorce, case lawyers agreed on a $4.8M settlement for me and possession of the ranch. I was anxious to discover where the money had gone.

Though the upgrade to low sulfur products would be, Juan felt, excessively expensive – estimates then for the conversion were at $15M - even though he had secured insurance money from a fire that burned down a shopping center he built and owned on the Navajo Reservation. He collected the insurance money and never rebuilt the shopping center. He liked doing business on the reservation, had a Navajo partner, and gas stations and convenience stores there, perhaps because it was a country unto itself and beyond US Law. He eventually told me about the fire and said it had been set by a rival. I had not heard about this event and was taken aback. Another of my brothers, Greg Hanson, built the laundromat with its colorful orange and yellow Wascomat machines, which were capable of washing something as large as a teepee. It seemed a loss for the Native Americans and a waste of resources.

That this brother had also designed and built a portable solar water purification unit, which Juan represented at trade shows as his own development, caused the first of several consequential rifts in our marriage. I had to insist that he not represent it as his own, and when this company sold with my brother's unit as the primary attraction, Juan told me what I now know was a fabricated story about the new owner losing his young wife and baby in childbirth. Juan said he felt sorry for him and did not pursue him for payment, hoping it would lead me to believe he had never gotten paid...

Tre's was given the Medical Power of Attorney by his dad to sign for him at the hospital when he got the hiccups during our heated discussion about why he had been given this authority, usually given to the wife - "I have given Tre's everything!" including Woody, the Percheron draft horse I had won several championships with and whom he had promised to me. Instead, he went to Tre's, who knew nothing about horses and didn't care about them...Juan left everything to Tre's and nothing to the rest of his children. This revelation was astounding!

I thought of the other three children, and my heart went out to them. They would be forever tied to a brother whom they loved but despised. As the favored child, Juan had made room additions to Tre's new home. He bought him a new Cessna 206 with a heads-up display and gave him the corporate reins, much to the chagrin of his other children. They spoke openly about these offenses; their father's actions may have made them reconsider their love.

That he would give this son, whom I had taught to fly, control of everything and his other children; nothing was a turning point for me. I did not wish to be controlled by Tre's or submissive, and when I made my objections, Juan rose to his full height, stood over me with his arms flailing, and screamed his directives in a way I had never seen or heard him do before. Suddenly, he got violent hiccups - which incapacitated him and landed him in the hospital for two weeks sometime before. I dropped the subject of our exchange and eased him into a chair, then stepped aside to make dinner preparations. When he had eaten and was calmer, I stepped outside onto the porch to call Tre's. "you have the medical power of attorney, and he needs to go to the hospital." Some hours later, Tre's arrived and the two conversed while I packed Juan's suitcase in a distant closet.

When Juan discovered that I was sending him away, he again became violent, and the hiccups returned. "She will really be sorry," he exploded in spotty words as he got into the car. I was transfixed by his departure, realizing I would probably never see him again. I fled to Phoenix in the night to be with a girlfriend of many years.

Carrie lived near the Biltmore Country Club, where Juan and I lived for several years. We were next door to the cotton farmer who turned his cotton ranch into the Phoenix International Raceway, Buddy Jobe, and across the street from Charles Magadini, civil and structural engineer who certified that my indoor regulation dressage arena north of Prescott in Sullivan Buttes would withstand 140 mph winds.

When Juan died a year later, Tre's called to un-invite me to the funeral and the elegant wake at Talking Rock, my country club. Few attended the burial, but my long-time foreman Tito was invited, went, and was astonished that Juan was planted in a homeless persons' cemetery. He related to me that Percheron Woody, my Woody, and Austin pulled the wagon carrying Juan in a cardboard box. There were no funeral arrangements, nor was the body embalmed. Juan was buried in the Odd Fellows Cemetery in what to this day is an unmarked grave.

At the sumptuous wake, in over 200 pictures of Juan's life, I never appeared. It was as if our marriage had never happened, and we had been together for nearly thirty years! When asked where I was, nothing was said except that we were divorcing. This and other experiences give me pause in my associations with men, and some twelve years later, I am without.

I had a luncheon memorial attended by about sixty of our friends. I wore purple. Then-friend Carrie gave an inspiring eulogy centered on Juan's optimism. When she left at the end of the luncheon, she told me she was going to attend Juan's wake at Talking Rock, instructing me that I was not welcome in her home or in her life. For what reason she reached this dismissal, I could not fathom, as I thought I had been to her the friend I thought she was to me. She could see that I was now without status or money to lend her as in the past.

A ROSEBUD SUNRISE

It was another glorious sunrise in Rosebud in 1934. A sunburst of pink and gold shafts illuminated the eastern horizon. Just before the golden ball ascended, Jim Wilson loaded the last bale of alfalfa onto his hay wagon, climbed up onto the driver's seat, and sorted out the reins, a weight of some twenty pounds when he took up contact with the horses' mouths. The fifteen-year-old spoke softly to the team of blacks who danced in their traces with anticipation: "Move on!" The Percherons got on the muscle to get the load moving, then picked up a steady jog along the dirt road and fell into a rhythm that made the whole rig swing and harnesses sing.

Feeding the stock started before dawn. Jim fed and harnessed the team, returned to the house for a quick breakfast, then went back outside to finish loading and hitching just as daylight came to the sky. With the taste of fresh biscuits, eggs, and bacon still in his mouth, Jim took his wagon over the rise toward the cattle while his dad went with his Clydesdales to do the same but in the opposite direction. It didn't take long to feed the 600 heads, and then it was back to the house to unhitch and be present for school when Miss Melody began lessons at eight.

The young teacher lived in an apartment in the Wilson home during the school year, took her meals with them, and left during the summers. Miss Melody had been there several years, and everything seemed to be working out okay, but Jim was restless and gazed out the windows a lot. His father, the grandson of Chief Crazy Horse of the Dakota Sioux, was a taskmaster. As Jim grew older, strict adherence to his father's regimen became a chore, but until he was a little older, he could only work and go to school and grow.

Jim's mother, Nellie Mae, was proud of her family and home. Near the Lakota reservation, but not on it, her family of seven children, all grown and gone except for Jim, the youngest, ranched and farmed for years in South Dakota, feeding their stock in winter from stores of hay grown in summer. Bigger, older ranching families built large homes like this one. The structure was of wood and adobe bricks varying from dark red to a light sand color. It was a single-story, ranch style, with long porches and a fireplace in nearly every room. There were seven bedrooms in the house, enough to accommodate the family, a teacher, and the occasional traveler or cattle buyer.

Furniture in the house was made of ash, a reddish brown in color. The seats of the chairs were cowhide. Jim's father went by James Wilson, but his native name was Walking Horse. He built his wife a dining room set of white oak held together by pegs, and it was her pride to polish until the wood gleamed. She had dishes of heavy crockery for everyday use, utensils of steel and pewter, a large set of fine china, and silver with an ornate pattern given to her by her husband and saved for special occasions. She polished the silver with heated, sour whole milk, submerging the silver in it until the tarnish disappeared, then set it in hot water until it shined. Her cookware was of steel or cast iron. Nellie Mae's favorite colors to use in the house were red and gray. Gray was easy to clean. She had a washing machine made from a wooden barrel with a drain hose in the bottom. The interior was corrugated to beat dirt out of clothes, and it oscillated by a stick cranked back and forth. Later, Jim's father used a gasoline engine to drive a belt, which agitated the handle automatically. Finally, the last machine Jim can remember was a square Maytag with a gasoline engine on the bottom to drive the agitator. Drained water was used in the garden. All these things eventually went to Jim's sister as part of her dowry.

Nellie Mae never cut her hair; it was long enough to sit on when she took it down. She oiled it with sage oil until it gleamed and wore it in braids or coils wrapped around her head. Her home was large and practical and served as protection against the South Dakota weather. There were four distinct seasons, each with a dynamic turn. Winters were roughest, with weeks of temperatures 25 to 30 degrees below zero. Jim walked or rode his horse to school in Rosebud, several miles away, and he went to school every day, regardless of the weather. Miss Melody also walked or rode a horse to school while staying with the Wilsons.

Nellie Mae milked her cow Bessie and sang softly to her as she pulled the pink teats. It was one of many tasks she completed each day. She cooked, cleaned, canned, baked, and sewed, in addition to tending a large garden. Two and a half acres were for vegetables and herbs. She raised corn, two or three different peas, and dried beans like great Northern, little whites, and butter beans. Her chickens hunted for bugs and worms, pecking around her feet while she picked, pruned, watered, and weeded. They liked to be around Nellie Mae while she worked in the garden. Five acres were in orchard trees, grown for canning fruits and dry stores such as potatoes. She made her favorite sauerkraut by fermenting cabbage with salt, pressed down inside a crock with a heavy board.

Fishing the streams for trout and hunting game supplemented their fare and pleasured the family with recreation. There were herds of antelope, whitetail deer, and elk. Smaller games consisted of jackrabbits, snow bunnies, sage hens, ducks, and geese.

This was the young life of Chief Jim Wilson, who left home at fifteen to join the US Army Calvary just at the end of the First World War.

ALICE

I see your body;
It lies in state.
Your face, pale and drawn

Your eyes are closed as not of late.
Your hair tousled, the luster gone.
Slippers of blue upon your feet

A dress of silk adorns your form.
Life's sweet mysteries now complete.
As laid to rest, your duties borne.

Those left behind will miss your smile.
The brightness of a countenance gay
Your loving touch,
your deeds worthwhile. Inevitably,
Revenge will find a way.

Now, thirteen steps complete the climb.
A hangman's noose will end this rhyme.

Alice, a poem written by Bliss Hanson in 1961, won Annandale High School's poetry writing contest in Fairfax County, Virginia, and consisted of a 14-line Sonnet written in Iambic Pentameter, ending in a couplet.

SAGITTARIUS

The hardest task, we always try.
A stairway reaching to the sky. We race with time
While seeking fame,
Above all else
We love the game!

-

Bliss

LEADER EMERGENCE

An inquiry into leader emergence

Throughout history, fascination with leader emergence has been the subject of theoretical, suppositional, and practical inquiry. Leaders may have the advantage, education, and opportunity, but leadership traits are gifts a person is born with, not earned. Consider the volumes profiling the world's leaders, the directions in which they led, and the consequences of their leadership. Literature portrays a leader's emergence from a group as a process that becomes nearly inseparable from what a leader does: lead.

Muchinsky (2006) presents six major areas of research interest in explaining leadership. First, there is positional power, which is concerned with the power of a position such as chief executive officer or president and denotes authority. Defining the character of the leader, who possesses certain characteristics and quality traits such as vision, decisiveness, and confidence, is a second area of research. A third area is the influence process, which involves the concept of attaining goals through coercion, manipulation, exertion of legitimate power, or persuasion.

The situation advances the idea that different situations require different leadership behaviors and may involve socially favorable or unfavorable behaviors in accomplishing these goals. Finally, leader emergence in opposition to leader effectiveness deals with comparing what makes a leader as opposed to how well a leader leads. Bridging these six research areas with a theoretical approach furthers the picture of how a leader emerges from a group. With a constellation of positive traits such as extraversion, tolerance for stress, optimism, drive, conscientiousness, and vision, the negatives of ambiguity and uncertainty would not be logical accompaniments.

The Trait approach, the oldest conception of leadership, addresses personality, but a more recent evolution of the same approach relates leader skills of technical expertise, conceptualization, and interpersonal cooperation. Specific behaviors conducive to the initiation of structure and the situational approach in which leadership occurs differently, situation to situation, appear synchronously. Exertion of power and influence by one person within a group is an attempt to get others to behave or react in a certain way. The leader/member exchange theory (LME theory) deals with the in-group where subordinates are differentiated by leaders according to their competence and skill, level of trust, and motivation. The path-to-goal theory relates to the situation where a leader customizes the path to the goal for subordinates. Transformational and charismatic leadership deals with changes in objectives and strategies, and leadership is an attribute divinely bestowed. Abandonment of leadership roles may occur in favor of substitutes or a more democratic process of direction and governance derived from role or task structuring, and finally, the implicit leadership theory suggests that a person regarded as a leader is held in esteem in the minds of the led, and is accorded power by acknowledgment.

Convergence from findings results in three consistent themes from these theories YUKL 1994: the importance of influencing and motivating, maintaining effective relationships, and the ability to make decisions. Add these to these perceptions, welding diverse interests and values, proficiency at balancing tasks, and the silhouette of a leader emerges.

Now, we are talking big leaders; onto the fun part. One characteristic distinctly missing from much of the literature I read is the analysis of personality whereby a leader gets his confidence and impetus to lead. Because the interpretation of character traits fundamental to the confidence found in those who lead is so mysterious, the origin of these notions is often attributed to the deliverance of powers and explained by acts of deity. Consider the sword, Excalibur, drawn from a large stone only by the young Arthur, soon to be king, or the flaming sword from the sky deposited into the hand of Attila the Hun. These are signs. With these acts comes a basis for leadership accepted as rightful by those led. In the minds of followers who attributed greatness to the receptor, the events are real. The evolution of these stories develop through the ages to become folklore.

Ancient accounts of leadership involve the potentate in a surrounding where s/he gleans insight into an understanding of human nature or vision illuminating the way. Whether this insight is sought or absorbed into the subconscious is inconsequential in the end, but it does approach again the question of whether leaders are born or made. Given the circumstances of King Arthur and Attila's rise to power through the touch of the deity, the symbolism is perpetuated by folklore. There has to be an explanation for why one individual rises to power and greatness when others do not, and the touched by god theory explains the unexplainable.

To read Margaret Thatcher's books, The Path to Power and The Downing Street Years, one might think leaders can be made. A verse by Henry Wadsworth Longfellow explains:

The heights by great men reached and kept Were not attained by sudden flight, but they, while their companions slept, were toiling upward in the night.

Margaret attributes the association with her parents as examples germane to the development of her articulate powers of observation, intellectual inquiry, and social concern.

These skills were recognized by them as important to survival and existence in pre-World War II England. Circumstances of her childhood, born of parents of industrious and contemplative natures, her father hailed from a long line of shoemakers, and her mother from dressmakers. They applied their skills to businesses in Grantham, England. Margaret was born in 1925 in their shops. She was preceded by a sister who did not share Margaret's zest for political life, nor did she accomplish similar innovation given the same upbringing. Through some act of nature, Margaret's degree of intellectual capacity was superior, but only in the sense that she was inclined to pursue her ambitions and capabilities even after marrying and giving birth to twins. Through adept organization, she multi-tasked: nurturing her little girl and boy, managing a household, running for her first political office that she did not win, and passing the bar exam within six months of giving birth. Margaret has a complex personality, and among her attributes, she has the qualities of a transformational and charismatic leader. Allowing for a leadership scale that assesses components of transformational leadership revealing association with work unit effectiveness as well as overall effectiveness, Bass (1997) advanced the idea that not only did the four components of transformational leadership transcend organizational and national borders with the concepts of idealized influence, inspirational motivation, intellectual stimulation, and individualized consideration, but it spoke to the universality of leadership. Perhaps, in some ways, Margaret's charisma was responsible for her rise even more than the transformational process of leading others in her stead. Ah, Mystical Charisma, a trait almost elusive in quality, harkens back to the oldest concepts of leadership: The Trait Approach.

Another woman with leadership qualities is recently retired Supreme Court Justice Sandra Day O'Connor. She portrayed her childhood days as filled with the hard work of ranch life. Having sold a substantial business in Oklahoma, her father took his profit as seed money to purchase large portions of land extending from New Mexico into Arizona and created the Lazy B Cattle Ranch, which is historically still the largest ranch in Arizona. Sandra's childhood was characterized by parental recognition and the development of her intellect through attendance at private schools, even though she still returned home to help on the ranch. Rather than the hard, physical work assigned to her brother and the cowboys, she was given chores ascribed to her gender, such as preparing and delivering lunch for the group via horseback somewhere out on the spread.

Sandra's brilliance gained her admission to Stanford Law School at sixteen, and eventually, she was appointed by Ronald Reagan as Supreme Court Justice, becoming the first woman to hold that position of power. Her situational approach to leadership, her decisions, and her votes have been viewed as moderate and characterized by the less governance, the better. In this week, April 16, 2007, of the Supreme Court Decision, without her, legislating morality by outlawing some aspects of abortion has again become women's reality. Her legitimate, expert, and referent power will be sorely missed.

In reading these portrayals, the common theme that runs through them is that their leadership abilities are not because they are children of privilege or that they were singled out over their siblings for greatness, but that somewhere in their personal make-up exists the innate desire to excel. Given intrinsic values possible for all children within their families, how else can superstardom be explained except through the burning bush or the bolt of lightning?

Leaders sometimes come from substantial families, even royalty. It would be easy to write of their greatness as leaders and attribute it to their breeding or inherited position, but that would be side-stepping the question. Consider Attila's 32 generations of Mongols descended from King Mundzuk of the Danube region west of the Urals in 395 A.D., or William of Wallace who led the Scotts against England for Scotland's independence, or Winston Churchill, descended from the Hapsburgs and substantial architect for defeat of another charismatic, though coercive leader of no particular lineage, Adolph Hitler.

The influence of family, an environment conducive to developing an inquiring mind through an atmosphere of security, love, and equanimity, and the development of an awareness of the society around them may contribute to the profusion of qualities and privilege. Overcoming barriers, as laid out by Dr. Paul Stoltz in his book, The Adversity Quotient: turning obstacles into opportunities or contending with a rule characterized by inefficiencies. Imagine being thrust into a strange foreign territory, such as Attila, as a child hostage. He saw his opportunity and made the most of it. Sent away to the Roman Court of Honorius by his Uncle Ruglia, successor to King Mundzuk's throne, Attila, at twelve years old, challenged Ruglia's power by speaking up at an assemblage of Chiefs. He announced opposition to Ruglia's entering the horde as mercenaries into foreign services of other nations he thought could easily be defeated. Lands and spoils were taken for the Huns. Attila envisioned a future of conquest for the Horde. This trait, vision, together with others' history, ascribed to his leadership abilities, are set down in Attila's writings. He had a fine perspective of leadership and power, to say nothing of his depth. He must have been a lonely man with all those Huns around.

While hostage of the Roman Court, he turned obstacles into opportunities when he finally resolved there was no escape. He learned all he could, and information was freely given because Rome knew these young hostages would carry this influence back to their homes, thus extending Roman influence into foreign nations as well as increasing the possibility of espionage. When Attila secured his leadership after catching the Burning Sword aboard Villan, his black war horse (coincidently, I have named a young black colt, similarly, Willum, without knowledge of the foregoing, which has no point other than they are both noble horses with coincidental sounding names), he visualized an empire which the conquest served to unite the errant, nomadic tribes of barbarians into a formidable force of some 700,000 warriors filled with esprit de corps! Attila possessed the traits to discipline, train, and lead his armies to conquer most of the civilized world. He abhorred weakness. He set forth certain principles by which a leader should live; these involved more of what a leader should do, Roberts, (1987).

Today, Attila would be an unpopular monarch, but many of the leadership qualities he wrote about are fundamental for explaining different theories. His leadership advice is studied in a primer for corporations entitled Leadership Secrets of Attila the Hun by Wess Roberts. After Attila, no leader emerged from the Huns – they probably couldn't find another one educated in Rome - and though several tried to keep them together as a horde, they fell back into tribes and resumed their nomadic lives.

> *One ship drives east, And another drives west,*
> *By the self-same gale that blows,*
> *'Tis the set of the sail, and not the gale,*
> *That determines the way she goes.*
>
> *Ella Wheeler Wilcox*

There has to be an explanation for how one individual can rise to greatness when others all around never do. The "touched by god" theory explains the unexplainable: leaders are born, not made.

ASSESSING THE INTERVIEW

The process known as the Interview has been in use for a long time, and except for additions and variations, nothing in history has proven as effective in the selection process. The intent of this paper is to show how an interview might be conducted, illustrate the content and manner of questioning, and assess the reliability and validity of the process.

The interview may range from the selection of an applicant to fill a position to a job analyst reviewing subject matter experts (SMEs) on the nature of their work. Gathering information on work to be done is instrumental in deciding what should be addressed when considering job applicants. Selecting SMES as individuals to relate information is germane to the process. S/he should be qualified to make informed judgment calls on the nature of their work. Included in the personal characteristics of SMEs are strong verbal abilities, sound memories, and a spirit of cooperation during the analyses.

While the analyst may have several motives in mind during the SME interview process, such as increasing job efficiency, creating less variance, therefore less waste, and establishing guidelines for hiring new personnel, it behooves her/him to explain to employees what the reason for the interview is, why it is important to the company to gain this information and the reasons for collecting it in the first place before observations and interviews begin.

It would be reciprocally important for employees to be reassured that they will not lose their jobs. If a job analyst's motives aren't made clear, employees may become frightened and fear for their jobs. This may result in the exaggeration of responsibilities and knowledge in an effort to save their jobs, resulting in contaminated data, which ultimately may be unusable. The time wasted and faulty information gathered would be a poor reflection of the job analyst's method of operation. Therefore, care should be taken while reviewing/ interviewing/addressing SMES.

Effectively completed, the job analyst's analysis should establish criteria for training, promotions, salaries, performance evaluations, and applicant selection. While the interview is widely used as a method of collecting information about the nature of processes, this aspect is now set aside in order to address the use of the interview in the applicant selection process.

There are several reasons hypothesized for the persistent use of the interview as a method of personnel selection (Arvey & Campion, 1982). The interview is a valid form of inquiry into the credentials and thought processes of the applicant. The possibility that the interviewer may make fallible judgment calls is only human (the Illusion of Validity, Muchinsky, p. 117) but is considered better than no assertion at all when taking into account the criteria of the selection process. Effective and desirable personality qualities may be sought, such as the ability to get along with others and conscientiousness. In order for more than one person to make the decision about selection, a panel of interviewers, each with a slightly different motive in mind, may be present and active.

Taking care that correct traits are sought during the interview, not choosing one applicant over the other because of extraversion, the ability to wow a panel, is addressed by Jane W. Moy in her study of this issue related in a 2006 article entitled: Are Employers Assessing the Right Traits in Hiring? (Evidenced from Hong Kong companies: International Journal of Human Resource Management, 17(4).

One effective type of interview is presenting the applicant with an issue and asking that they suggest how it should be resolved. Some interviewers revolve around this situational context and draw from what the applicant knows to solve future hypothetical problems. This scenario deals with the highest level of learning – working from the known to the unknown, taking knowledge, and applying it to a new situation with a resulting successful outcome: application of the highest level of learning.

Another type of interview is the experience-based interview. Researched by Pulakos and Schmidt (1995), this scenario slightly changes the focus of the interview to questions based on experience and situational solutions. The motivation of employees assigned distasteful but necessary tasks plays a central role in management employment considerations. Interviewers may have key thoughts in mind while listening to solutions, but it is a judgment call on her/his part as to whether the criteria are satisfied or added to by the answers. Multidimensional answers, whether discussed in person or by recording or telephone interviews, include the distinctions of taking initiative and solving problems. As an additional benefit, selling the applicant on the value of the job and the attractiveness of the organization is an added bonus and amounts to starting the new employee off on the right foot.

Assessing the predictive and criterion-related validity of the employment interview in my line of work follows. First, the goal of psychological assessment is to know something about the individual for the purpose of making an inference about that person's ability to perform a job well. That something could range from ambition to emotion to skills. Industrial/organizational (IO) psychologists have developed predictive measures designed to aid in decision-making in the selection process. These predictors deal with forecasting skills. Evaluating past professional behavior, testing, and interviewing are all designed to foresee professional behaviors. Predictors, whether they be through testing or interviews, are designed to forecast future employee success.

In my present line of work - and I have had others - I am in the business of breeding, raising, training, and selling warm-blood sport horses. They are given a foundation of dressage (a form of riding which translated from French means training). Dressage is the fundamental execution of movements of the horse and horsemanship by the rider, where the animal is ridden in complete harmony. The two appear to dance. Dressage is the foundation and the end-point for every other kind of riding, from jumping to cross country.)

My experience covers the last 23 years. I have consistently worked on the variables over time and continue to progress in degrees. It is a most challenging business. I am presently in need of an additional trainer. We are in the process of hiring an individual, having completed several face-to-face, in-depth interviews. The remaining test is the actual riding of two horses: one experienced and one inexperienced horse. The interview panel consists of four people intimately involved in our day-to-day operation. They are also trainers and have a vested interest in the selection process since they will be working closely with the applicant.

Based on the acceptable answers to questions asked so far during the interview, the applicant's degree of expertise will be evidenced in today's riding. Predicting how well-trained these horses will be by this new trainer is a combination of attitude, experience, and skill in riding dressage. As we sell these horses for a nice sum, the selection of a skilled trainer is paramount.

During the interview process, I have kept in mind the degree to which predictors differ in qualities, realizing that this has been the subject of extensive research in IO psychology. Four guidelines have been suggested by R.B. Kennedy in his article published in the Journal of Employment Counseling, 31(3) - the employment interview. Keep bias and error out of the interview to delete contamination. With so many ethnic applicants, take a worldly view and appreciate the ambition and what it took for the applicant to get to this point (learning English, immigrating, getting a work permit or Green Card). Embrace the differences in cultures.

Establish predictors that are reliable, with results consistent over time, which can be gleaned during the interview. For example, asking for references and then checking those references - with stables in Germany, which is this woman's native country - by getting their summation and recommendations of her abilities is one way to predict the outcome of her training. Asking for information from previous employers about her training methodology is a way to assure me of her capabilities and techniques.

Assessing the dimensions of her knowledge, skills, and approach to her training during the interview process (AKSAO - knowledge, skills, abilities, and other) by presenting several what-if actual scenarios we have going on in the barn reveals results consistent with her past record, and serve as valid indicators or predictors of success in her new job. (We presented the following scenarios: (1) we have one young horse who was bitten in the nose by a rattlesnake and now bites everything and everyone.

(2) We have a high-strung mare coming back from stepping on a long screw, and she is difficult because she has a medical memory of the pain. (3) We have another horse who goes bananas every time she is presented with a new situation or setting.) Enduring abstract constructs of motivation, adaptability, intelligence, and drive criteria, together with the objective construct of her

physical skills compared with my own and the other trainers, measure during the interview process what they are supposed to measure: her ability to do the job of training horses well.

She is a lovely young woman, tall and athletic, and is educated in horsemanship and other things from German schools. She is fluent in English, which is good as I am not fluent in German. She is married to an American and has a year-old child. She pursued this job after having her baby, who will be in the care of a sitter three afternoons a week. I have seen her ride in the past; she is a lovely rider, so I am sure of her ability. With this predictor in mind, I am sure she will treat the job and the horses carefully. She lives locally, perhaps only a 15-minute drive from my facility, and presents herself well with positive answers and compassion for the animals. My present prediction is that she will show herself well in the saddle, and we will hire her. I feel that the interview has been fair, socially acceptable, and legally sound, and her hiring is within our cost and time constraints. We have mutually decided upon her salary.

The interview has been a useful tool in determining the most effective way for both the applicant and my organization to assess whether or not we will marry. Using situational scenarios presented by a panel of interviewers and listening closely to the answers are good predictors of how successful the applicant will be. Whether the interview is conducted telephonically, videoed, or, most desirably, in person, it is a process of selection improved upon over time but not replaced. The conclusion is that we believe we have hired the correct individual for the job.

LEADERSHIP

Four topics that relate to leadership are presented in the following annotations. Assessing teaching excellence among professors involves conceptual criteria that measure a theoretical and ideal standard of teaching excellence. Defined by goodness, thoroughness, intellectual capacity, and professionalism, these canons are not unlike qualities sought in leadership positions. Goodness, thoroughness, and intellectual capacity refer to the Trait Approach to leadership, the oldest conception of leadership, where the notion of common sense is an amalgamation of these traits. The Behavioral Approach to leadership corresponds to professionalism in that it shifts the focus from specific traits leaders possess to actions leaders engage in behavior. Professionalism involves being knowledgeable, timely, and prepared, seeking further growth, and having an appreciation for other points of view. Characteristics embodied by professionalism would be ideal in a leader. In Maslow's human need hierarchy, self-actualization is the highest level of human progression. After needs fundamental to good physical and mental health are met, personal fulfillment is sought. This high-level drive results in positive work motivation, behavior towards accomplishment, and observable performance, all features sought in a leader. Three distinct motivational traits are personal mastery (a combination of initially hypothesized personal mastery and hard work traits), competitive excellence, and achievement and failure avoidance traits. Analyses and research findings by Heggestad and Kanfer (2000) support the development of motivational skills in purposeful undertakings such as leadership. Extra discretionary contributions within an organization that is neither required nor expected is a phenomenon termed organizational citizenship behavior. Five-dimensional behaviors supported by experiential research (LePine, Erez, & Johnson, 2002), which translate directly to desirable leadership behaviors, are altruism, conscientiousness, courtesy, sportsmanship, and civic virtue. These prosocial behaviors are highly valued as long as they are a genuine reflection of intention and not merely self-serving (Bolino, 1999).

The Self-Protective leadership style is an example of a leadership style that might be termed self-serving and is found in cultures where collectivism, large power distance, uncertainty avoidance, and disparate gender roles would be found. In contrast, prosocial behavior is a phenomenon termed organizational deviance or workplace incivility, which investigates antisocial behaviors. Evidenced by insults, threats, lying, theft, sabotage, physical violence, and occupational homicide occurring in the workplace, the underlying reason for these behaviors is to exact revenge from an organization that is perceived to be unjust. Frequently, there are reports of workplace shootings in the news. Taken to another level, the leadership level, exacting revenge can result in an abuse of power represented by the Power and Influence Approach taxonomy of coercion.

The best leader I have been directly connected with and influenced by was the Director of Flight Academics during my tenure at Embry Riddle Aeronautical University, Prescott, Arizona, campus. First, his leadership abilities were evidenced by the trait approach to power because of the dynamics of his personality. He had the ability to persuade the powers that be in Finance to get additional funding for our department when there was little allocation for any department. Other traits such as decisiveness, extraversion, and assertiveness won him the respect of all at the university.

His power and influence approach over his department was evidenced by his use of legitimate, expert, and referent powers in the conduct of the department. He had legitimate power to assign classes to us as teachers. He had expert power derived from his career as an air force fighter pilot. His piloting skills were extraordinary, and he consistently traded the title of International Aerobatic Champion with the Flight Department Head, his best friend, in their Pitts Special biplanes, year-to-year. His degrees were in aeronautical engineering, design aerodynamics, and education. He displayed referent power because he possessed character qualities of confidence, vision, and sophistication, connoting an appeal to staff and students alike. He led the way for us to be a powerhouse within the university because we knew that our jobs were fundamental to the knowledge base required of all flight students, and he set an example of the highest level of teaching by presenting ideas via constructs of illustration of his points. He was our implicit leader in that we emulated him as he was accorded such impetus and importance in our minds. He supported the path-goal theory approach to leadership and made us aware of specific expectations of the mission, enabled us to do our jobs better by providing constructive support, and allowed us to participate in decisions empowering and trusting us, thereby enhancing the psychological contract we maintained with the university, and set high standards for our achievement as teachers. On a beautiful Sunday afternoon, witnesses saw two biplanes touch wingtips during a dogfight at 300 feet. The university has not recovered from this loss.

Collectivism, large power distance, uncertainty avoidance, and disparate gender roles could be found in contrast to prosocial behavior, and a phenomenon termed organizational deviance or workplace incivility investigates antisocial behaviors. Evidenced by insults, threats, lying, theft, sabotage, physical violence, and occupational homicide occurring in the workplace, the underlying reason for these behaviors is to exact revenge from an organization that is perceived to be unjust. Frequently, there are reports of workplace shootings in the news. Taken to another level, the leadership level, exacting revenge can result in an abuse of power represented by the power and influence approach taxonomy of coercion.

A situation where authoritarian leadership may work well would be in a machine shop, a maintenance base, a military force, or in a country where the level of intellectualism is low. When satisfying basic needs such as obtaining food and shelter does not leave much energy for contemplation of lofty ideals. Cultures where collectivism, large power distance, uncertainty avoidance, and disparate gender roles are prevalent would be where authoritarianism reigns. Look at tumultuous Africa. The idea of empowerment may be a lost cause in that some people just don't comprehend the vision, direction, or strategy required; there is no psychological contract because it is impossible to comprehend. The examples of situations given here could find improvement if they joined the information age by accessing and learning to use computers (an entrepreneur in India has come out with a PC selling for $125 using seven-year-old, discarded, but still good, power units). The development of the personal computer has been the single most significant factor in improving communications, making more constructive use of time, and increasing awareness. When this happens, the world may change, and the idea of authoritarian power will be a thing of the past.

"AUTHORITY WITHOUT WISDOM IS LIKE A HEAVY AXE WITHOUT AN EDGE, FITTER TO BRUISE THAN POLISH."

Anne Bradstreet

Muchinsky (2006) presents six major areas of research interest in explaining leadership. First, there is Positional Power, which is concerned with the power of a position such as Chief Executive Officer or President and denotes authority. Defining the character of The Leader, who possesses certain characteristics and quality traits such as vision, decisiveness, and confidence, is a second area of research. A third area is The Influence Process, which involves the concept of attaining goals through coercion, manipulation, exertion of legitimate power, or persuasion. The Situation advances the idea that different situations require different leadership behaviors and may involve socially favorable or unfavorable behaviors in accomplishing goals. Finally, Leader Emergence in opposition to Leader Effectiveness deals with comparing what makes a leader as opposed to how well a leader leads. Bridging these six research areas with a theoretical approach furthers the picture of how a leader emerges from a group. With a constellation of positive traits such as extraversion, tolerance for stress, optimism, drive, conscientiousness, and vision, the negatives of ambiguity and uncertainty would not be logical accompaniments.

The Trait Approach, the oldest conception of leadership, addresses personality, but a more recent evolution of the same approach relates leader skills of technical expertise, conceptualization, and interpersonal cooperation. Specific Behaviors conducive to the initiation of structure and the Situational Approach in which leadership occurs differently, situation to situation, appear synchronously. Exertion of Power and Influence by one person within a group is an attempt to get others to behave or react in a certain way. The Leader/Member Exchange Theory (LMX Theory) deals with the in-group where subordinates are differentiated by leaders according to their competence and skill, level of trust, and motivation. The Path-Goal Theory relates to the situation where a leader customizes the path to the goal for subordinates. Transformational and

53

Charismatic Leadership deals with changes in objectives and strategies, and leadership is an attribute divinely bestowed. Abandonment of leadership roles may occur in favor of Substitutes or a more democratic process of direction and governance derived from role or task structuring, and finally, the Implicit Leadership Theory suggests that a person regarded as a leader is held in esteem in the minds of the led, and is accorded power by acknowledgment.

Convergence from findings results in three consistent themes from these theories, Yukl (1994): the importance of influencing and motivating, maintaining effective relationships, and the ability to make decisions. Add these perceptions welding diverse interests and values, proficiency at balancing tasks, and the silhouette of a leader emerges.

Now, we are talking big leaders; onto the fun part. One characteristic distinctly missing from much of the literature I read is the analysis of personality whereby a leader gets his confidence and impetus to lead. Because the interpretation of character traits fundamental to the confidence found in those who lead is so mysterious, the origin of these notions is often attributed to the deliverance of powers and explained by acts of deity. Consider the sword, Excalibur, drawn from a large stone only by the young Arthur, soon to be king, or the flaming sword from the sky deposited into the hand of Attila the Hun. These are signs. With these acts comes a basis for leadership accepted as rightful by those led. In the minds of followers who attributed greatness to the receptor, the events are real. The evolution of these stories developed through the ages to become folklore.

Ancient accounts of leadership involve the potentate in a surrounding where s/he gleans insight into an understanding of human nature or vision illuminating the way. Whether this insight is sought or absorbed into the subconscious is inconsequential in the end, but it does approach again the question of whether leaders are born or made. Given the circumstances of King Arthur and Attila's rise to power through a touch of the deity, the symbolism is perpetuated by folklore. There has to be an explanation for why one individual rises to power and greatness when others do not, and the touched by God theory explains the unexplainable.

To read Margaret Thatcher's books, The Path to Power and The Downing Street Years, one might think leaders can be made. A verse by Henry Wadsworth Longfellow explains:

> *The heights of great men reached and kept*
> *Were not attained by sudden flight,*
> *But they, while their companions slept,*
> *We were toiling upward in the night.*

Replacing an authoritarian style would be a democratic style where employees are empowered, the psychological contract is acknowledged, computers are used, and the age of information is alive through Internet access. People in individualistic cultures are most apt to demand democratic governance, where they have a say in leadership, direction, path, and goals. First, my leadership would be tailored to the completion of the tasks or project and would be termed situational leadership. I would look to see before I led. Then, I would acknowledge the workforce's strengths and weaknesses. My philosophy in governance and direction would be a combination of several approaches. Using the transformational approach, I would implement the four inspirational tenets of idealized influence where I would conduct myself as a model for subordinates, giving inspirational motivation along with intellectual stimulation in reframing problems and individual consideration to the wants and needs of workers appropriate to the work setting. Once I got to know my people, and they, me, I would implement the LMX theory of leader/member exchange in that with reliance on the loyalty of workers and their perceived competence in me, there would be an established psychological basis for the exchange, and ultimately, an organization which could go forward and do work accomplishing anything. It is thought that a good example of one of the best-run companies in the world is the conglomerate of General Electric (GE), where employees are either slated for advancement or for exit. Applying the theory of Six Sigma to its organization of attendant companies, GE has sought to reduce variance, thereby reducing waste. I would seek to reduce waste.

Also, a company that stagnates produces waste and needs to be refreshed. Six Sigma is directed toward improving processes that organizations use to meet their customers' needs. A closer look at the five critical phases of process improvement would be to define the needs of customers, measure variables, analyze the problems associated with production and delivery, improve the processes through potential solutions, and control process performance at a desired level. The end result of all this speculation of what kind of a leader I would be is that I would implement timely and appropriate philosophies of leadership and, once underway, strive for constant process improvement with the least variance and no waste. The psychological basis underlying the LMX Theory (leader/member exchange) accentuates the importance of leader behavior not just toward the group as a whole but toward individuals on a personal basis. Research evidence maintains that behaviors such as trust, loyalty, open communications, mutual respect, and commitment to success are the foundations of a constructive exchange. If this psychological checklist is addressed by leadership, the outcome of an organization that uses this basis for operations will find success. The importance of the psychological contract between employer and employee cannot be emphasized enough. Though usually unwritten, satisfaction with the psychological contract is the underlying reason why people stay with an organization, and violation of it is the reason they leave. It is the reason I left Delta Air Lines seven years early and the reason I left Embry Riddle University after only two and half years of teaching. More on this first incident in my books entitled Air Affair and Air Affair II.

According to Bojes & Rhodes (2006), the transformational leader of McDonald's in and around 2003 was Jim Cantalupo, CEO and Chairman, who resurrected the flailing company and returned its stock to profitability until his death in 2004. After him, two successive leaders, Charlie Bell, and Jim Skinner, continued the leadership transformation beset by many challenges of the day: blunting attacks that McDonald's served unhealthy food, changing the public's idea that healthy food/lifestyle was now its thrust, and by providing a menu of natural foods. Given McDonald's organizational context known for efficiency and standardization more than for adaption (Ritzer, 1993/2002) under the leadership of founder Ray Kroc, and considering their franchises around the world, it would be tempting to see McDonald's as unreceptive to change wrought by transformational leadership, but voila`! Key to this transformation has been the critical leadership function of the comic icon Ronald McDonald, born in the era of McDonald's less bureaucratized marketing and advertising departments in the early days. Ronald has enabled the organization to respond to the challenge of change. McDonald's uses Ronald as a means of energetically transmitting its corporate strategy and changing location agendas. There are 250 official Ronalds in the United States who espouse a double narration: the corporate litany and through the interpretation of one of the oldest vehicles of mirth: a clown who promotes the new McDonald's image as the world's largest restaurateur who envisions now being seen as a health conscious, fitness-oriented organization. Though somewhat constrained by upper management, Ronald's ability to speak back to corporate management through his lampoons has been found to be pivotal in analyzing McDonald's culture and its ultimate transformation into a modern-minded conglomerate of fast-food restaurants. The new category of leader for McDonald's is embodied in the svelte, smooth-talking Ronald, who conducts physical workouts in the parking lot and espouses a healthy outlook on life.

HERWIG

Herwig Glander was introduced to me via Terri Tugman, my dressage instructor from Hawaii. I took dressage lessons from her every Saturday on layovers in Honolulu while flying as second-in-command on the elegant Lockheed 1011 Tri-Star for Delta Air Lines. Terri lived on her mountain ranch north of Honolulu on the ocean side of Oahu with views of the Omega antennae farm, which looked like spider webbing attached to the mountains. Before satellite navigation and global positioning navigation systems, the Omega systems took their triangulations from the antennae spread across the mountains.

I met Terri when she judged a three-day event I was competing in north of Salt Lake City at the fairgrounds with my big, dark quarter horse show-named "Sweet William, naw, Wild Bill!" Terri placed me first after Stadium Jumping. After this event, I invited Terri to judge my Zephyr Ranch Horse Trials in Spanish Fork, and that is when she mentioned I should use Herwig Glander as my dressage instructor for an advanced horse named Dante` I was buying from Olympian Stefan Peters. Herwig was originally from Germany via Canada and was invited by the Church of Latter Day Saints to be an honorary German Consul as he was fluent in the languages of Europe and Russia, and he was practicing law.

Herwig came to me for lessons at a friend's place, which reduced the distance he had to drive from his law offices north of Salt Lake City. He drove his economical little Honda Civic, which had the front seats removed so Herwig could get his 6'7"+ frame seated comfortably on the rear seat. His tall height limited his competitive dressage ambition, so he gave dressage lessons instead, sometimes on one of the dark Russian Trakehners he kept at home.

My Dante` was a naughty boy and did not like doing what Herwig asked, as he was accustomed to more experienced riders than me. Throughout the next several years, the horse and I became friends, but his joy was trail riding

58

in the mountains of Arizona. Eventually, we sold our ranch in Spanish Fork to Elizabeth Smart's grandfather. He was a dairy farmer who owned eleven dairies around Utah and turned them into real estate developments. He wanted our picturesque ranch for his family gatherings. Each time we met, he raised the offered price until I knew I would never be able to sell for more. I sold, and we moved to Arizona.

I asked Herwig to come south, and he drove the distance in his Civic to give dressage lessons, judge, and clinic at the Northern Arizona Dressage Club activities. Once, he stayed with us at our house, which had all the doors removed for structural repair, new hardware, and painting. It was a chummy experience.

Herwig confided to me that he was in Hitler's navy, commanding a submarine at 24 years old. I was stunned by this revelation. I knew that German boys were inducted into the military and asked how he felt being a Nazi? His comment was: "There are two sides to a war, and someone has to be on the losing one." And that was that.

I have always wondered - but never asked - if he sailed his submarine up the St. Lawrence River, sunk it, and immigrated to Canada. There is a lot of speculation about the Nazi leaders sailing in subs to South America, but Herwig did not like the hot, humid weather there. The Perones of Argentina were friends with Hitler, and he was their benefactor. Watching programs exploring jungles and mountains where mysterious mansions have been found - usually built to take advantage of lakes and waterways – I never believed that Hitler committed suicide in a bunker with his lover, Eva Braun, though history leads us to believe so. I think he was too clever; he sailed in a submarine to South America and lived the life of a rich man in a beautiful mansion far from his country of origin.

OUR HORSES ARE OUR FRIENDS

"There is something about the outside of a horse that is good for the inside of a man," President Theodore Roosevelt has often been quoted as saying. Horsemen and horsewomen can relate to this as the time spent with our equine friends transcends our everyday cares. Step inside your barn to hear soft sounds of munching hay, shuffling feet, and groans of pleasure. Soft whinnies greet us as heads rise in acknowledgment of our approach. We are invited to step into another world, if we will, a world where time slows and energy flows.

The interval spent astride can be inspiring, addicting, or, it can be an ill-afforded distraction. When our horse's companionship and willingness are eclipsed when we no longer have the desire to make time to spend with them, what will we do? Can we give them away to a friend whom we hope will care for them as we have? We wish we could sell, but perhaps the market is not there. We would like to somehow recover the time and expense we have spent on them. But what price has pleasure?

The level of kindness and humanity is illustrated by the manner in which people keep and treat their animals. And when we are finished with them, when we feel we can no longer keep them, our humanity should awaken a sense of responsibility to see that they are looked after as friends. Before giving up and consigning them to an auction and worse, there are alternatives to explore. There are many rescues where the horses are kept ready for adoption. One such place is in Kanab, Utah, close to the Arizona border, called Best Friends. It takes in and cares for all kinds of animals.

There are schools and camps which gratefully accept horses and consider them as donations. In the past, I have given several horses to the Brigham Young

University Equestrian Program. Having introduced three-day events to that area years ago with Zephyr Ranch Horse Trials, the university elected to include this discipline in its equestrian program. They were thrilled to have experienced three-day horses donated. There are also many equestrian programs in Arizona schools and colleges that may welcome horses.

Another place that accepts horses is the Chauncey Ranch in Maher, just off Highway 69. The ranch is about 4,000 acres and grows its own hay. The children's equestrian program is operated by the YMCA in Phoenix and employs an experienced equine staff. I made contact through a telephone call to Phoenix. They sent a large trailer. Half of my older horses are now in their program and live happily out in a grassy field protected by hills. They are teaching children to care for and ride on the many trails. I can visit my horses whenever I want. There are alternatives available for the future of our equine friends. As responsible horsemen, with inquiry and effort, a humanitarian solution can be found for relocation.

PERPETRATORS

I am living in the shade of the Nevada Sierras on my beautiful ranch, raising horses, cows, and chickens, and writing creatively. The weather is always a factor – so different from my old stomping grounds in the Yavapai County of Northern Arizona, where yearly temperatures varied by less than twenty degrees. This variation has caused much physical stress, making walking a challenge, especially on uneven ground.

A large horse I was riding there suddenly died and fell with me under him, causing head injuries and hairline fractures in my extremities. It was indeed a life changing event as I lost my medical certification and I was a professional pilot! The altitude is something I am accustomed to though not the humidity - nor soaring and plunging barometric pressures.

So why would I move here? I moved here because I needed to get away from an area where I was known as the wife of a wealthy man and move to a different place where a favorite brother with a large family lived nearby. The mountains are utopic especially now that they are partly snow-covered and one can see through to dark vegetation.

My ranch is in the middle of the Carson Valley and, being centered, basks in sunlight all day until late. I live near the small towns of Minden and Gardnerville whose population is 48% seniors. With a dirt road leading to the ranch which assures cows can be safely driven up and down, it also affords a bit of security as people with nice cars refrain from driving on it. Lake Tahoe is just up Kingsbury Grade over the Sierras.

Heavy lifting of bales of hay and tree trimming fall on my brother, who is large and strong. He says he enjoys working the ranch. He does a nice job with the grounds, but there was a time when I thought I was going to have another husband who could care for all that and me.

Eight years ago, I began playing online Scrabble with Leonardo Walker Crockett and Words with Friends with Smith Williams. They lived and worked on different oil rigs for Shell Oil of The Hague offshore in the North Sea near Scotland. Both were Sub Sea Engineers. Their earnings were kept inaccessible in savings accounts at Gateway Bank in Edinburgh until their contracts were terminated. So they looked to wealthy widows and offered 20% to take part in their Cartel's romantic schemes.

They sounded reasonable, but Google warned that if the mention of money was made, the game – Scrabble and WWF would cease, so Leonardo asked that we Chat on an App called Hang Outs, then later on Google Chat, and finally using WhatsApp. Smith William did basically the same. Both turned out to be Perpetrating a money-seeking affair promising romance. I ended up losing their promised 20% and much, much more.

2009

A stunning year! Ranging afar

Diving islands of French Polynesia
Zip-lining Panama with friends
Rafting the Grand Canyon Commercial fishing in Alaska waters
Healthy at last!
Seven new lovebirds
Another great-grandson.
Tender, the loving heart Oden, the Wolfhound, a Hanoverian colt
A gray Welsh pony and a brown one, too A Percheron hitch
Writing Classes
Air Affair, my first book,
Calming Rough Waters,
Reminiscing in Glowing Coals,
Fondly reflecting on friendships
Of many years

-

Bliss Knight

ADVENTURING SPIRIT

Bliss Knight

For as long as I can remember, I have wanted to be a writer, but I needed some life experience to write about. When I was a young girl, the eldest daughter of a colonel who was heading up the testing of missiles and rockets for the Army's Arctic Test Branch at Big Delta, Alaska, there was no television. Alaska wasn't even a state yet, so I read... about far-off places in books like Gunga Din, Marco Polo, and Bomba the Jungle Boy. I found that I yearned to see the world.

I looked out windows at the clouds and the sky and dreamed of the independence and freedom learning to fly would offer. Seeing my dad off on yet another Pan Am Boeing 337 and the flight crews with their worldly expressions and fine uniforms - accented by reveres on the women's lapels made me wonder about their experiences. So, at the tender age of nine, I decided then that I would become an International Airline Pilot, which would give me some things to write about. Pursuing this goal gave my life purpose, definition, and direction.

Living in a one-room log cabin, then, without the amenities of running water or indoor plumbing, we bathed once a week in a galvanized tub, all in the same water Dad brought from the Post in five-gallon Jerry cans. This was embarrassing for a prepubescent girl. We had light from a single bulb when the generator would start, but when it wouldn't, I did my homework with a kerosene lantern. Attending a one-room territorial school in the early 1950s, I listened carefully to what the older children were learning.

My mother had a rare skin condition, like Poison Ivy, which precluded her from putting her hands in water. I knew when I stepped off the Army Personnel Carrier from school that dishes and diapers were waiting. I built a fire each evening to heat water using only the allotted single match, even in the wind, to wash dishes and diapers, and bathe my little brothers.

As I scrubbed, my mind's eye wandered, yearning for another life and not one so regulated but freer. When we saw my dad off on yet another Pan Am flight to the lower 48 states, I wished I could fly along. The crew's expressions evidenced their worldliness, and I wished I could fly along with them... So, at the tender age of nine, I developed a yearning to fly, which carried me through. I never missed a chance to fly with members of the Aero Club or our Episcopal Bishop.

I found that I wanted - not children - but horses in numbers. Black Beauty was among my favorite books. My mother always said that Horse was my middle name. It wasn't really. My middle name is Bliss, the one I go by. I was named after an Army Post in El Paso, Texas, called Fort Bliss. I guess it is good that I wasn't born in Ft. Huachuca...

At sixteen, I flew an airplane solo, then progressed through the ratings, eventually instructing for Flight Safety International, whose motto was: "The best safety device in any airplane is a well-trained pilot." I was happy to be flying there for years.

I have been married two times, the first time to an air tanker pilot who flew Grumman TBMs on fires and the Lockheed Electra carrying the San Diego Padres Baseball team to games. Together, we flew Smoke Jumpers and repossessed big airplanes. We went to college at the University of California at Berkeley with our earnings. Our marriage ended when he could not endure that I had been hired by Western Airlines - the first commercial airline in the USA - as one of the first female pilots. It was very hard being attentive in classes, knowing my husband was living with another woman.

My second marriage ten years later was to a businessman who had a refinery and a fleet of corporate airplanes: an Aerostar, King Airs, and a Westwind jet, to name a few. He also loved boats. Early in our marriage, we built an elegant houseboat to use on Lake Powell. I couldn't figure out how to raise children well when always away flying, so I have birds, cats, dogs, horses, and friends...My animals have special names that describe their personalities: Green Meadow Bear, a Newfoundland, Odessa and Grizzi, Irish Wolfhounds, and Leo, an Anatolian Shepherd who protects my grazing animals from predators. Tiara, a Hanoverian mare for Dressage. Leidi, a white Arab for trail riding. And a miniature horse, Buttercup, for driving carriages. Benson is my black Angus bull, and with him, his many consorts.

Life has had a lot of firsts for me. I was a first child. I flew out of San Francisco for one of the first Air Ambulance companies airlifting patients and medical teams in a Cessna 414 for Stanford and the University of California Hospitals. I was the first woman Smoke Jumper pilot (Dehaviland 300 Twin Otter) and Air Tanker pilot (Lockheed P2V-5 Neptune) with an Initial Attack Rating on contract to the USFS. I instructed professional flight engineers of Pan American Airways, Seaboard World Airlines, Flying Tigers, and American Airlines for their pilot's licenses at Flight Safety International. I flew and instructed for several airlines: Japan Air Lines, Scenic Airlines, Western Airlines, and Delta Air Lines as one of the first women pilots, and I retired from Delta as a Captain. I got to fly the elegant Lockheed 1011 Tri-Star internationally. My dream of seeing the world realized, flying has allowed me to visit other countries and cultures and see many natural wonders such as the icebergs calving off Greenland's southern tip, Hayley's Comet clearly through the night while flying to Europe, and the whole Grand Canyon, 217 miles of it from east to west, spectacular at sunrise and at sunset!

Appointed as an FAA Designated Pilot Examiner, I administered flight tests and issued most flying licenses, including Flight Instructor, Multi-Engine, and Airline Transport Pilot. I taught first at Cerritos College in Southern California, then Embry Riddle Aeronautical University Aviation Academics Department in Prescott, Arizona, and was offered the position of Department Head after one month by the late Professors Robert Swegginis and Mike Corradi of aerial dogfighting fame.

I have written about my adventures in aviation in my first book, Air Affair, and in my second book, entitled Air Affair II. Both are available through Amazon, Barnes & Noble, and other bookstores. The advent of online accredited classes allowed me to complete my Bachelor's Degree from the Old Dominion University in Norfolk, Virginia, which began as a part of our oldest college, William and Mary, and separated to begin teaching Nautical Engineering -

Shipbuilding. In 2014, I received my Master's Degree in Business from Western Governors University and was selected to give the keynote speech during our Graduation Ceremony, available on YouTube. Online education is absolutely the most innovative and best idea in gaining an education ever!

I developed a 501.C3 non-profit called Aqua Sun Foundation for my brother Greg Hanson as my Capstone Project for my MBA, obtaining tax-exempt status for his donors. The organization constructs solar water purification units to send to disaster-ridden and needy areas of the world. Shortly after, I put together a for-profit marketing business called SAM (an acronym for Superior American Marketing).

I took early retirement from Delta for a couple of reasons: the first being they retired my favorite airplane, the Lockheed 1011 Tri-Star, for safety reasons – it was structurally unsound. After 35 years in service, the flight deck separated in flight from the cabin of their oldest 1011. Held on only by stringers, with 10 inches of blue sky showing in the gaping circle and missing one unfortunate flight attendant not strapped in during depressurization, the aircraft landed safely in Honolulu, never to be used again. Lockheed loaded it aboard a ship and sailed it home for research. The 1011 airplanes were retired to lie about in the deserts.

Another reason I took early retirement was I was given an opportunity by my husband to sail his yachts up and down the Inland Passage between Juneau and Seattle. I got my Coast Guard Masters License for ships, attending Clatsop College with him located in Astoria, a city in Oregon at the confluence of the Columbia River and Pacific Ocean. With the ship's logs in hand, the Coast Guard qualified us to Captain inland and offshore vessels.

I write on my laptop computer set up with a view of the Sierras around Lake Tahoe and of my pastures within view of my Black Angus cows grazing. When the wind is blowing over the mountains, and it is a cloudy day, a phenomenon of the Sierras, standing Waves form, sending Lenticular clouds far past the lee side of the mountains, inviting soaring enthusiasts from around the world.

FLYING AIR TANKERS
AND THE ROBOTIC AI

T here was an FBO (Fixed Base Operation) called Minden Air, built and owned by Len Parker, a crop duster at the Minden Tahoe Airport originally from the Tucson area. I used to see his airplanes dusting while driving cross country with carriages in competition. He had a successful business flying dusters for 26 years before deciding to move to the Carson Valley in Northern Nevada and fly air tankers to put out forest fires. That there are no state income taxes in Nevada, a phenomenon that attracts business ventures, sealed the deal.

He set up shop at Minden in several hangars and operated the Lockheed P2V Neptune as air tankers on contracts. They put out forest fires in and around Lake Tahoe. For many years, he operated the P2V on U.S. Forest Service contracts until a transition to *jet* delivery of the red fire retardants visible from the air - FosCheck and FireStall - became inevitable.

The P2V was being readied for retirement as it was initially developed as a pure reconnaissance seaplane during WW 11, the Korean and Viet Nam Wars. With its two compounded radial engines and two jet engines for assistance during action, it was a successful air tanker.

Minden Air began preparing several BAE 146s to replace the aging P2Vs. Day and night, they worked for several years, adding retardant tanks and delivery systems to the BAE 146 jets.

I met the Chief Pilot at the Minden Airport in the summer of 2012 when he was looking to hire experienced jet pilots with a background in fire fighting. I retired as a jet Captain with Delta Airlines; and got my Initial Attack Rating on Fires for Evergreen International from the U.S. Forest Service in 1981 – the first woman qualified to do so in the world. I flew Smoke Jumpers into forests for Intermountain Aviation (a predecessor of Evergreen International) with DeHavilland Twin Otters and was thinking of relocating from Prescott, Arizona, to Northern Nevada, where I had a younger brother with a large family.

In 2013, I completed my Master's Degree in Business from Western Governors University, an online University founded by 17 Western State governors (where I gave the keynote speech at graduation, now online in a U Tube presentation.)

After the ceremony in Salt Lake City and back home the next day in Prescott, a large Dressage horse I was riding dropped dead on top of me. If he had gone down to the left, I could have just stepped off, but he went down to the right, and his body fell on top of my head and extremities. My foreman was near, saw what happened, and had motionless me whisked away by helicopter to Flagstaff Hospital.

I spent one and a half days unconscious, undergoing tests. Besides the head injury, I had hairline fractures of several bones in my body. Doctors there said I would *only take time to heal*. Then, I was released to a Good Samaritan Convalescent home in Prescott and transported there by ambulance from Flagstaff. As I was recently widowed and there was no one at home to help me, I remained in Good Sam's care for two months until I was released under my own recognizance to go home, where my two white Irish Wolfhounds sweetly crawled out on their stomachs to greet me. I made a note of the difference between a *hospital* – where they *cut* - and a *convalescent* facility – where they give *care during convalescence*.

I remained in a doctor's care and engaged in physical therapy. On the anniversary each year of the accident, I had X-rays and an MRI to confirm my healing progress. Several times, I presented for medical certification both in Prescott and Reno, receiving positive feedback *and* my medical certification to fly.

Knowing I might have a job flying air tankers for Minden Air and hoping to leave familiar ground I had walked on for seventeen years with my late husband, which now only made me blue, I decided to sell in 2015. Keeping only a few horses to ride on my new, smaller ranch in Nevada. It, too, had an indoor arena along with stunning views of the Sierras.

The US Forest Service then awarded contracts to an outfit that operated 4 Douglas DC-10s out of Goodyear, Phoenix, Arizona as air tankers, and Minden Air, with its two smaller BAE 146 jets, was left out. Len Parker fought the good fight to no avail and abandoned his project and property, leaving the whole place in disarray for years until Douglas County got after him to clean it up.

The next time I presented for medical certification, I was denied by the new Artificial Intelligence of IACRA as I had not included my Good Sam *convalescent stay* as *hospitalization*. Hospitalization of two months or more was grounds for medical certificate denial. But Good Sam is not a hospital.

I wrote to the FAA explaining that a two-month *convalescent stay* was the *care given* as I was widowed and had no one at home to care for me, that a *hospital could cut,* and that cutting was not deemed necessary in my case. I was told by the AI of IACRA – the web-based online application process which stands for Integrated Airman Certification and Rating Application - that I would be sorry if I challenged this decision because my exclusion of the convalescent facility in the application process amounted to lying on a federal form, an anomaly which could result in federal imprisonment.

I wrote to attorney Jim Hales, who had won several cases for me, but he was on an extended vacation in Europe, so I had no one I trusted to dispute this life-changing decision. IACRA's AI had not given credence to the mission or difference between a *hospital* where they *cut* and a *convalescent home* where they *heal. That I should be denied medical certification, which I previously held successfully for many years, because of a technicality – hospital vs. convalescent facility – is unforgivable!* As I could not engage with Hales, I dropped the subject and now do not fly anything.

ECHOES OF LIFE

Bliss and Juan

Bliss and Leo

Bliss

Inland Passage Sailing

Odessa

Bliss & Juan with Lilly at
Grass Ridge

Juneau, Alaska

Grizzi, Irish Wolfhound,
Odessa's father

Bliss and mare Laurel

Miniature pony Buttercup

Bliss and Happy Hour

Percherons Woody & Austin at
Hitch in competition

Lockheed 1011 Tri Star
turning to land at Maui

My Home

Aero Star

Bliss and Freedom

Tally

Tally, Bliss and Juan in Grass Ridge

Front doors of our home

Our Lake

REFERENCES

Chomsky, N. (2006). Survey of the Brain: as others see us. The Economist, 12/23/2006-01/05/2007, 9.

Furnham, A., Burbeck, E., (1989). Employment interview outcomes as a function of the Interviewer's Experience. Perceptual and motor skills, 69 (2), 395-402.

Kennedy, R. B. (1994). The Employment Interview. Journal of Employment Counseling, 31(3), 110-114.

Moy, j. W. (2006). Are employers assessing the right traits in hiring? Evidence from Hong Kong companies. International Journal of Human Resources Management, 17(4), 734-754.

Muchinsky, P.M. (2006). Psychology Applied to Work, eighth edition, 66, 98, 115-118, 303.

Purkiss, S. L., Segrist, P., Gillespie, T.I. (2006). Implicit sources of bias in employment interview judgments and decisions. Organizational behaviors and human decision processes, 101 (2), 152-167.

Saks, A. M., McCarthy, J. M. (2006). Effects of discriminating interview questions and gender on applicant reactions. Journal of business and psychology, 21(2),175-191.

Bateman, T.S., and S.A. Snell, Management. Seventh edition, McGraw-Hill/Irwin Publishing, Boston, p. 264, 374, 402, 408.

Boje, D.M., and Rhodes, C., The Leadership of Ronald McDonald: Double narration and stylistic lines of transformation. The Leadership Quarterly, 17(2006), 94-103.

Galbraitih, J.K., (1967). The New Industrial State. Houghton, Mifflin Company, Boston, p. 57-98.

Muchinsky, P.M., (2006). Psychology Applied to Work, eighth edition, Thomson/Wadsworth Publishers, Belmont, California, p. 58, 80, 339, 384, 431.

Thatcher, M., (1995). The Path to Power. Harper Collins, Publishers, New York, p. 3-101, 282-329, 565-601.

Bateman, T.S., and S.A. Snell, Management. Seventh edition, McGraw-Hill/Irwin

Publishing, New York, p. 264, 374, 402, 408.

Day-O'Connor, S., (2002). Lazy B. Random House Publisher, New York.

Galbraitih, J.K., (1967). The New Industrial State. Houghton, Mifflin Company,

Boston, p. 57-98.

Muchinsky, P.M., (2006). Psychology Applied to Work. Eighth edition,

Thomson/Wadsworth Publishers, Belmont, California, p.58, 80, 339, 384, 431.

Roberts, W., (1985). Leadership Secrets of Attila the Hun. Warner Books Publisher,

New York.

Stoltz, P., (1997). Adversity Quotient: Turning Obstacles into Opportunities.

Wiley Publishing, Los Angeles.

Stoltz, P., (2000, 2001). Adversity Quotient@ Work. Morrow Publishing, New York.

Thatcher, M., (1993). The Downing Street Years. Harper Collins Publishers, New York, p. 173-235.

Thatcher, M., (1995). The Path to Power. Harper Collins, Publishers, New York, p. 3-

101, 282-329, 565-601.

www.ingramcontent.com/pod-product-compliance
Lightning Source LLC
Chambersburg PA
CBHW051232120626
46547CB00013B/1606

* 9 7 9 8 8 9 3 2 4 4 0 3 8 *